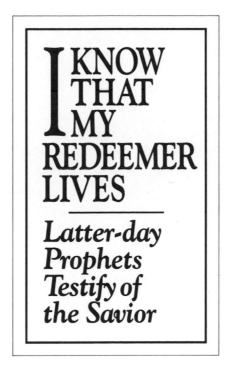

I KNOW THAT MY REDEEMER LIVES

Latter-day Prophets Testify of the Savior

Deseret Book Company
Salt Lake City, Utah

Portions of the quotations and writings contained in chapters eight through thirteen are used by permission of The Church of Jesus Christ of Latter-day Saints.

Cover design by Brent Christison. Cover illustration taken from "Christ and the Rich Young Man" by Heinrich Hoffman © The Church of Jesus Christ of Latter-day Saints. Used by permission.

Library of Congress Cataloging-in-Publication Data

I know that my redeemer lives.
    p. cm.
  Includes index.
  ISBN 0-87579-388-6 (hard)
    1. Jesus Christ—Mormon interpretations. 2. Spiritual life—
Mormon authors.
  BX8643.J4I25 1990
  232—dc20   90-45780
                                               CIP

Printed in the United States of America

10   9   8   7   6   5   4   3   2   1

CONTENTS

v

vi

PUBLISHER'S PREFACE

All thirteen latter-day prophets have proclaimed that Jesus is the Christ, the Son of God. All have shared their witness of the Lord and Savior with the world. While all have testified of his greatness and glory, all have also contrasted his majesty with the individual attention he showers on each of his Father's children. All have emphasized that Christlike acts, constant living of his commandments, and emphasis on service and sincerity are what convince the soul that Jesus Christ lives.

Though today's latter-day prophets have no need for signs, they have received them. As they have prepared themselves for life eternal, the Lord has prepared them for final service at the head of this church — under his direction. Hence prophets have been schooled in the ways of the Lord through their own living. They have had disappointments and disasters beyond the scope of many; they have had to reach for an understanding of principles; and they have had to build their commitment to God's plan, precept upon precept. Their testimonies are poignant and to the point.

In one general conference, Elder Boyd K. Packer explained the responsibility of being a special witness of Jesus Christ: "We do not talk of those sacred interviews that qualify the servants of the Lord to bear a special witness of Him, for we have been commanded not to do so.

"But we are free, indeed, we are obliged, to bear that special witness." (In Conference Report, April 1980, p. 86.)

Often, such witness comes not of fire and thunder but of the still, small voice speaking softly to the soul. The prophets tell of those quiet moments when they alone wrestled with the weight of their role and found new comfort in the Redeemer, who suffered for all mankind. From the witnesses of these prophets, it is clear that testimonies are determined not by what we say but by how we live.

Preparation of this book involved reviewing all the conference talks given by those who became presidents of the Church, the *Journal of Discourses,* and many talks from funeral sermons to seminary graduation addresses to letters to family members. Messages in the church magazines, printed compilations of addresses and thoughts, newspapers, biographies, and journals were consistent source material for each prophet. Citations follow the excerpts selected for publication. Except where otherwise indicated, the author of the source is the prophet of the chapter.

These sources do not exhaust all that the prophets have said in testifying of the divinity of Jesus Christ. Rather they highlight significant passages either testifying of the Savior or teaching about some aspect of the Savior and his eternal ministry. Some of the longer passages have been condensed because of space limitations. Deletions between sections are indicated by ellipses.

The testimonies of the prophets are not loaded with expansive terms and flowery phrases. Instead, their references to and sermons about the Savior are intimate and reverent. One prophet's statement capsulizes the relationship of the Lord to his prophets: "He is my friend, my Savior, my Lord, my God." This compilation reflects that relationship.

Chapter 1

JOSEPH SMITH, JR.

Born: 23 December 1805
Ordained an apostle: May 1829
Sustained as president of the High Priesthood: 25 January 1832
Died: 27 June 1844

THE FIRST VISION. I was one day reading the Epistle of James, first chapter and fifth verse, which reads: *If any of you lack wisdom, let him ask of God, that giveth to all men liberally, and upbraideth not; and it shall be given him.*

Never did any passage of scripture come with more power to the heart of man than this did at this time to mine. It seemed to enter with great force into every feeling of my heart. I reflected on it again and again, knowing that if any person needed wisdom from God, I did; for how to act I did not know, and unless I could get more wisdom than I then had, I would never know; for the teachers of religion of the different sects understood the same passages of scripture so differently

1

as to destroy all confidence in settling the question by an appeal to the Bible.

At length I came to the conclusion that I must either remain in darkness and confusion, or else I must do as James directs, that is, ask of God. I at length came to the determination to "ask of God," concluding that if he gave wisdom to them that lacked wisdom, and would give liberally, and not upbraid, I might venture.

So, in accordance with this, my determination to ask of God, I retired to the woods to make the attempt. It was on the morning of a beautiful, clear day, early in the spring of eighteen hundred and twenty. It was the first time in my life that I had made such an attempt, for amidst all my anxieties I had never as yet made the attempt to pray vocally.

After I had retired to the place where I had previously designed to go, having looked around me, and finding myself alone, I kneeled down and began to offer up the desires of my heart to God. I had scarcely done so, when immediately I was seized upon by some power which entirely overcame me, and had such an astonishing influence over me as to bind my tongue so that I could not speak. Thick darkness gathered around me, and it seemed to me for a time as if I were doomed to sudden destruction.

But, exerting all my powers to call upon God to deliver me out of the power of this enemy which had seized upon me, and at the very moment when I was ready to sink into despair and abandon myself to destruction — not to an imaginary ruin, but to the power of some actual being from the unseen world, who had such marvelous power as I had never before felt in any being — just at this moment of great alarm, I saw a pillar of light exactly over my head, above the brightness of the sun, which descended gradually until it fell upon me.

It no sooner appeared than I found myself delivered from the enemy which held me bound. When the light rested upon me I saw two Personages, whose brightness and glory defy all description, standing above me in the air. One of them spake unto me, calling me by name and said, pointing to the other — *This is My Beloved Son. Hear Him!*

My object in going to inquire of the Lord was to know which of all the sects was right, that I might know which to join. No sooner, therefore, did I get possession of myself, so as to be able to speak, than I asked the Personages who stood above me in the light, which of all the sects was right (for at this time it had never entered into my heart that all were wrong) — and which I should join.

I was answered that I must join none of them, for they were all wrong; and the Personage who addressed me said that all their creeds were an abomination in his sight; that those professors were all corrupt; that: "they draw near to me with their lips, but their hearts are far from me, they teach for doctrines the commandments of men, having a form of godliness, but they deny the power thereof."

He again forbade me to join with any of them; and many other things did he say unto me, which I cannot write at this time. When I came to myself again, I found myself lying on my back, looking up into heaven. When the light had departed, I had no strength; but soon recovering in some degree, I went home. . . .

I had actually seen a light, and in the midst of that light I saw two Personages, and they did in reality speak to me; and though I was hated and persecuted for saying that I had seen a vision, yet it was true; and while they were persecuting me, reviling me, and speaking all manner of evil against me falsely for so saying, I was led to say in my heart: Why persecute me for telling the truth? I have actually seen a vision; and who am I that I can withstand God, or why does the world think to make me deny what I have actually seen? For I had seen a vision; I knew it, and I knew that God knew it, and I could not deny it, neither dared I do it; at least I knew that by so doing I would offend God, and come under condemnation.

—*Joseph Smith—History 1:11–20, 25.*

THE ADVOCATE WITH THE FATHER. Hearken, O ye people of my church, to whom the kingdom has been given; hearken ye and give ear to him who laid the foundation of the earth, who made the heavens and all the hosts thereof, and by whom all things were made which live, and move, and have a being. And again I say, hearken unto my voice, lest death shall overtake you; in an hour when ye think not the summer shall be past, and the harvest ended, and your souls not saved.

Listen to him who is the advocate with the Father, who is pleading your cause before him—saying: Father, behold the sufferings and death of him who did no sin, in whom thou wast well pleased; behold the blood of thy Son which was shed, the blood of him whom thou gavest that thyself might be glorified; wherefore, Father, spare these my brethren that believe on my name, that they may come unto me and have everlasting life.

Hearken, O ye people of my church, and ye elders listen together, and hear my voice while it is called today, and harden not your hearts; for verily I say unto you that I am Alpha and Omega, the beginning and the end, the light and the life of the world—a light that shineth in darkness and the darkness comprehendeth it not. I came unto mine own, and mine own received me not; but unto as many as received me gave I power to do many miracles, and to become the sons of God; and even unto them that believed on my name gave I power to obtain eternal life.

—*Revelation given through President Joseph Smith, Jr., 7 March 1831, in Doctrine and Covenants 45:1–8.*

THE SAVIOR HAS BEEN IN YOUR MIDST. At a meeting

held in the Prophet's home shortly after moving to Kirtland, a twelve-year-old girl and her mother were in attendance. After prayer and singing [the Prophet] began to talk. Mary Elizabeth Lightner was sitting on a plank resting on boxes. She watched the Prophet closely.

"Suddenly he stopped speaking and seemed almost transfixed. He was looking ahead, and his face outshone the candle which was on a shelf just behind him. I thought I could almost see his cheekbones. He looked as though a search light was inside his face. After a short time he looked at us very solemnly and said, 'Brothers and Sisters do you know who has been in your midst this night?' One of the Smith family said, 'An Angel of the Lord.' Joseph did not answer. Martin Harris was sitting at the Prophet's feet on a box. He slid to his knees and said, 'I know it was the Lord and Savior Jesus Christ.' Joseph put his hand on Martin's head and answered: 'Martin, God revealed that to you. Brothers and Sisters, the Savior has been in your midst. I want you to remember it.' "

—*Diary of Mary Elizabeth Lightner*, p. 4., *as recorded in Ivan J. Barrett,* Joseph Smith, an American Prophet: Great Moments in the Life of Joseph Smith, *Brigham Young University Lecture Series, (Provo, Utah: Extension Publications, 1963), p. 15.*

WHEN HE SHALL COME. When I contemplate the rapidity with which the great and glorious day of the coming of the Son of Man advances, when He shall come to receive His Saints unto Himself, where they shall dwell in His presence, and be crowned with glory and immortality; when I consider that soon the heavens are to be shaken, and the earth tremble and reel to and fro; and that the heavens are to be unfolded as a scroll when it is rolled up; and that every mountain and island are to flee away, I cry out in my heart, What manner of persons ought we to be in all holy conversation and godliness!

You remember the testimony which I bore in the name of the Lord Jesus, concerning the great work which He has brought forth in the last days. You know my manner of communication, how that in weakness and simplicity, I declared to you what the Lord had brought forth by the ministering of His holy angels to me for this generation. I pray that the Lord may enable you to treasure these things in your mind, for I know that His Spirit will bear testimony to all who seek diligently after knowledge from Him. I hope you will search the Scriptures to see whether these things are not also consistent with those things which the ancient Prophets and Apostles have written.

—History of The Church of Jesus Christ of Latter-day Saints, *ed. B. H. Roberts, 7 vols. (Salt Lake City: The Church of Jesus Christ of Latter-day Saints, 1951), 1:442.*

VISION OF THE FATHER AND SON ON THE THRONE. The heavens were opened upon us, and I beheld the celestial kingdom of God, and the glory thereof, whether in the body or out I cannot tell. I saw the transcendent beauty of the gate through which the heirs of that kingdom will enter, which was like unto circling flames of fire; also the blazing throne of God, whereon was seated the Father and the Son. I saw the beautiful streets of that kingdom, which had the appearance of being paved with gold. . . .

Thus came the voice of the Lord unto me, saying: All who have died without a knowledge of this gospel, who would have received it if they had been permitted to tarry, shall be heirs of the celestial kingdom of God; also all that shall die henceforth without a knowledge of it, who would have received it with all their hearts, shall be heirs of that kingdom; for I, the Lord, will judge all men according to their works, according to the desire of their hearts.

—*Doctrine and Covenants 137:1–4, 7–9.*

VISION OF THE LORD IN THE TEMPLE. In the after-
noon, I assisted the other Presidents in distributing the Lord's
Supper to the Church, receiving it from the Twelve, whose
privilege it was to officiate at the sacred desk this day. After
having performed this service to my brethren, I retired to the
pulpit, the veils being dropped, and bowed myself, with Oliver
Cowdery, in solemn and silent prayer. After rising from prayer,
the following vision was opened to both of us. . . .

The veil was taken from our minds, and the eyes of our
understanding were opened. We saw the Lord standing upon
the breastwork of the pulpit, before us; and under his feet was
a paved work of pure gold, in color like amber.

His eyes were as a flame of fire; the hair of his head was
white like the pure snow; his countenance shone above the
brightness of the sun; and his voice was as the sound of the
rushing of great waters, even the voice of Jehovah, saying: I
am the first and the last; I am he who liveth, I am he who
was slain; I am your advocate with the Father.

Behold, your sins are forgiven you; you are clean before
me; therefore, lift up your heads and rejoice. Let the hearts
of your brethren rejoice, and let the hearts of all my people
rejoice, who have, with their might, built this house to my
name.

For behold, I have accepted this house, and my name shall
be here; and I will manifest myself to my people in mercy in
this house. Yea, I will appear unto my servants, and speak
unto them with mine own voice, if my people will keep my
commandments, and do not pollute this holy house.

Yea the hearts of thousands and tens of thousands shall
greatly rejoice in consequence of the blessings which shall be
poured out, and the endowment with which my servants have
been endowed in this house. And the fame of this house shall
spread to foreign lands; and this is the beginning of the blessing

which shall be poured out upon the heads of my people. Even so. Amen.

—History of the Church, 2:435; Doctrine and Covenants 110:1–10.

BELIEF IN JESUS CHRIST. We believe in God, the Eternal Father, and in His Son, Jesus Christ, and in the Holy Ghost. . . . We believe that through the Atonement of Christ, all mankind may be saved, by obedience to the laws and ordinances of the Gospel. We believe that the first [principle] . . . of the Gospel [is]: first, Faith in the Lord Jesus Christ.

—Articles of Faith 1, 3–4.

IN THE NAME OF JESUS CHRIST. On the morning of the 22nd of July, 1839, he [the Prophet] arose, reflecting upon the situation of the Saints of God in their persecutions and afflictions. He called upon the Lord in prayer, the power of God rested upon him mightily, and as Jesus healed all the sick around Him in His day, so Joseph, the Prophet of God, healed all around on this occasion. He healed all in his house and dooryard; then, in company with Sidney Rigdon and several of the Twelve, went among the sick lying on the bank of the river, where he commanded them in a loud voice, in the name of Jesus Christ, to rise and be made whole, and they were all healed. When he had healed all on the east side of the river that were sick, he and his companions crossed the Mississippi River in a ferry-boat to the west side, where we were, at Montrose. The first house they went into was President Brigham Young's. He was sick on his bed at the time. The Prophet went into his house and healed him, and they all came out together.

As they were passing by my door, Brother Joseph said: "Brother Woodruff, follow me." These were the only words spoken by any of the company from the time they left Brother

Brigham's house till they crossed the public square, and entered Brother Fordham's house. Brother Fordham had been dying for an hour, and we expected each minute would be his last. I felt the spirit of God that was overpowering His Prophet. When we entered the house, Brother Joseph walked up to Brother Fordham and took him by the right hand, his left hand holding his hat. He saw that Brother Fordham's eyes were glazed, and that he was speechless and unconscious.

After taking his hand, he looked down into the dying man's face and said:

"Brother Fordham, do you not know me?"

At first there was no reply, but we all could see the effect of the spirit of God resting on the afflicted man. Joseph again spoke:

"Elijah, do you not know me?"

With a low whisper Brother Fordham answered, "Yes."

The Prophet then said:

"Have you not faith to be healed?"

The answer, which was a little plainer than before, was: "I am afraid it is too late; if you had come sooner, I think I might have been."

He had the appearance of a man waking from sleep; it was the sleep of death. Joseph then said: "Do you believe that Jesus is the Christ?"

"I do, Brother Joseph," was the response. Then the Prophet of God spoke with a loud voice as in the majesty of Jehovah:

"Elijah, I command you, in the name of Jesus of Nazareth, to arise and be made whole."

The words of the Prophet were not like the words of man, but like the voice of God. It seemed to me that the house shook on its foundation. Elijah Fordham leaped from his bed like a man raised from the dead. A healthy color came to his face, and life was manifested in every act. His feet had been done up in Indian meal poultices; he kicked these off his feet,

scattered the contents, then called for his clothes and put
them on. He asked for a bowl of bread and milk, and ate it.
He then put on his hat and followed us into the street, to
visit others who were sick.

—*Matthais F. Cowley*, Wilford Woodruff, History of His Life and
Labors, as Recorded in His Daily Journals *(Salt Lake City: Deseret News
Press, 1909), 104–5.*

FACE TO FACE. After any portion of the human family are
made acquainted with the important fact that there is a God,
who has created and does uphold all things, the extent of
their knowledge respecting his character and glory will depend
upon their diligence and faithfulness in seeking after him,
until, like Enoch, the brother of Jared, and Moses, they shall
obtain faith in God, and power with him to behold him face
to face."

—Lectures on Faith *(Salt Lake City: Deseret Book Company, 1985),*
2:55.

THE SECOND COMFORTER. There are two Comforters
spoke of. One is the Holy Ghost, the same as given on the
day of Pentecost, and that all Saints receive after faith, repentance, and baptism. This first Comforter or Holy Ghost
has no other effect than pure intelligence. . . .

The other Comforter spoken of is a subject of great interest,
and perhaps understood by few of this generation. After a
person has faith in Christ, repents of his sins, and is baptized
for the remission of his sins and receives the Holy Ghost, (by
the laying on of hands), which is the first Comforter, then
let him continue to humble himself before God, hungering
and thirsting after righteousness, and living by every word of
God, and the Lord will soon say unto him, Son, thou shalt
be exalted. When the Lord has thoroughly proved him, and
finds that the man is determined to serve Him at all hazards,

then the man will find his calling and his election made sure, then it will be his privilege to receive the other Comforter, which the Lord hath promised the Saints, as is recorded in the testimony of St. John, in the 14th chapter, from the 12th to the 27th verses. . . .

"I will pray the Father, and He shall give you another Comforter, that he may abide with you for ever; . . . and I will love him, and will manifest myself to him; . . . and my Father will love him, and we will come unto him, and make our abode with him."

Now what is this other Comforter? It is no more nor less than the Lord Jesus Christ Himself; and this is the sum and substance of the whole matter; that when any man obtains this last Comforter, he will have the personage of Jesus Christ to attend him, or appear unto him from time to time, and even He will manifest the Father unto him, and they will take up their abode with him, and the visions of the heavens will be opened unto him, and the Lord will teach him face to face, and he may have a perfect knowledge of the mysteries of the Kingdom of God; and this is the state and place the ancient Saints arrived at when they had such glorious visions — Isaiah, Ezekiel, John upon the Isle of Patmos, St. Paul in the three heavens, and all the Saints who held communion with the general assembly and Church of the First Born.

—History of the Church, 3:380–81.

THE LORD WAS NOT IN THE THUNDER. The manifestations of the gift of the Holy Ghost, the ministering of angels, or the development of the power, majesty or glory of God were very seldom manifested publicly, and that generally to the people of God, as to the Israelites; but most generally when angels have come or God has revealed Himself, it has been to individuals in private, in their chamber; in the wilderness or fields, and that generally without noise or tumult.

The angel delivered Peter out of prison in the dead of night; came to Paul unobserved by the rest of the crew; appeared to Mary and Elizabeth without the knowledge of others; spoke to John the Baptist whilst the people around were ignorant of it.

When Elisha saw the chariots of Israel and the horsemen thereof, it was unknown to others. When the Lord appeared to Abraham it was at his tent door; when the angels went to Lot, no person knew them but himself, which was the case probably with Abraham and his wife; when the Lord appeared to Moses, it was in the burning bush, in the tabernacle, or in the mountain top; when Elijah was taken in a chariot of fire, it was unobserved by the world; and when he was in a cleft of a rock, there was loud thunder, but the Lord was not in the thunder; there was an earthquake, but the Lord was not in the earthquake; and then there was a still small voice, which was the voice of the Lord, saying, "What doest thou hear, Elijah?"

The Lord cannot always be known by the thunder of His voice, by the display of His glory or by the manifestation of His power; and those that are the most anxious to see these things, are the least prepared to meet them, and were the Lord to manifest His power as He did to the children of Israel, such characters would be the first to say, "Let not the Lord speak any more, lest we His people die."

—History of the Church, 5:30–31.

WHO IS THE SON OF GOD? The Son, who was in the bosom of the Father, [is] a personage of tabernacle, made or fashioned like unto man, or being in the form and likeness of man, or rather man was formed after his likeness and in his image; he is also the express image and likeness of the personage of the Father, possessing all the fullness of the Father, or the same fullness with the Father; being begotten

of him, and ordained from before the foundation of the world
to be a propitiation for the sins of all those who should believe
on his name, and is called the Son because of the flesh, and
descended in suffering below that which man can suffer; or,
in other words, suffered greater sufferings, and was exposed
to more powerful contradictions than any man can be. But,
notwithstanding all this, he kept the law of God, and remained
without sin, showing thereby that it is in the power of man
to keep the law and remain also without sin; and also, that
by him a righteous judgment might come upon all flesh, and
that all who walk not in the law of God may justly be con-
demned by the law, and have no excuse for their sins. And
he being the Only Begotten of the Father, full of grace and
truth, and having overcome, received a fullness of the glory
of the Father. . . .

The saints have a sure foundation laid for the exercise of
faith unto life and salvation, through the atonement and
mediation of Jesus Christ; by whose blood they have a forgiveness of sins, and also a sure reward laid up for them in
heaven, even that of partaking of the fullness of the Father
and the Son through the Spirit. As the Son partakes of the
fullness of the Father through the Spirit, so the saints are, by
the same Spirit, to be partakers of the same fullness, to enjoy
the same glory; for as the Father and the Son are one, so, in
like manner, the saints are to be one in them. Through the
love of the Father, the mediation of Jesus Christ, and the gift
of the Holy Spirit, they are to be heirs of God, and joint heirs
with Jesus Christ.

—Lectures on Faith, 59–61.

THE MISSION OF THE MESSIAH. The spirit of Elias is
first, Elijah second, and Messiah last. Elias is a forerunner to
prepare the way, and the spirit and power of Elijah is to come
after, holding the keys of power, building the Temple to the

capstone, placing the seals of the Melchisedec Priesthood upon the house of Israel, and making all things ready; then Messiah comes to His Temple, which is last of all.

Messiah is above the spirit and power of Elijah, for He made the world, and was that spiritual rock unto Moses in the wilderness. Elijah was to come and prepare the way and build up the kingdom before the coming of the great day of the Lord, although the spirit of Elias might begin it.

I have asked of the Lord concerning His coming; and while asking the Lord, He gave a sign and said, "In the days of Noah I set a bow in the heavens as a sign and token that in any year that the bow should be seen the Lord would not come; but there should be seed time and harvest during that year; but whenever you see the bow withdrawn, it shall be a token that there shall be famine, pestilence, and great distress among the nations, and that the coming of the Messiah is not far distant.

But I will take the responsibility upon myself to prophesy in the name of the Lord, that Christ will not come this year, . . . for we have seen the bow; and I also prophesy, in the name of the Lord, that Christ will not come in forty years; and if God ever spoke by my mouth, He will not come in that length of time. Brethren, when you go home, write this down, that it may be remembered.

Jesus Christ never did reveal to any man the precise time that He would come. Go and read the Scriptures, and you cannot find anything that specifies the exact hour He would come; and all that say so are false teachers.

—History of the Church, 6:254.

SACRIFICE. For a man to lay down his all, his character and reputation, his honor, and applause, his good name among men, his houses, his lands, his brothers and sisters, his wife and children, and even his own life also—counting all things but filth and dross for the excellency of the knowledge of Jesus Christ — requires more than mere belief or supposition that he is doing the will of God; but actual knowledge, realizing that, when these sufferings are ended, he will enter into eternal rest; and be a partaker of the glory of God.

— Lectures on Faith, 6:5.

OUR TESTIMONY, LAST OF ALL. We, Joseph Smith, Jun., and Sidney Rigdon, being in the Spirit on the sixteenth day of February, in the year of our Lord one thousand eight hundred and thirty-two — by the power of the Spirit our eyes were opened and our understandings were enlightened, so as to see and understand the things of God — even those things which were from the beginning before the world was, which were ordained of the Father, through his Only Begotten Son, who was in the bosom of the Father, even from the beginning; of whom we bear record; and the record which we bear is the fulness of the gospel of Jesus Christ, who is the Son, whom we saw and with whom we conversed in the heavenly vision.

For while we were doing the work of translation, which the Lord had appointed unto us, we came to the twenty-ninth verse of the fifth chapter of John, which was given unto us as follows — speaking of the resurrection of the dead, concerning those who shall hear the voice of the Son of Man: And shall come forth; they who have done good, in the resurrection of the just; and they who have done evil, in the resurrection of the unjust.

Now this caused us to marvel, for it was given unto us of the Spirit. And while we meditated upon these things, the Lord touched the eyes of our understandings and they were opened, and the glory of the Lord shone round about. And we beheld the glory of the Son, on the right hand of the Father, and received of his fulness; and saw the holy angels, and them who are sanctified before his throne, worshiping God, and the Lamb, who worship him forever and ever.

And now, after the many testimonies which have been given of him, this is the testimony, last of all, which we give of him: That he lives! For we saw him, even on the right hand of God; and we heard the voice bearing record that he is the Only Begotten of the Father — that by him, and through him, and of him, the worlds are and were created, and the inhabitants thereof are begotten sons and daughters unto God.

   —*Doctrine and Covenants 76:11–24.*

Chapter 2

BRIGHAM YOUNG

Born: 1 June 1801
Ordained an apostle: 14 February 1835
Sustained as president: 27 December 1847
Died: 29 August 1877

HE IS MY MASTER. What shall we say, will not Jesus reign and subdue the world? Is he not the Saviour of the world, and the only-begotten Son of the Father, and will he not accomplish the work he came to accomplish? Is not the earth the Lord's, the wheat, the fine flour, the gold, the silver, the earth and all its fulness? Can you imagine to yourselves anything that pertains to this earth that does not belong to its Redeemer? He is my master, my elder brother. He is the character I look to, and the one I try to serve to the best of my ability. Should I not be proud of my religion? I think if pride can at all be indulged in, the Latter-day Saints should be proud.

    —11 July 1852, Journal of Discourses, 26 vols. (London: Latter-day Saints' Book Depot, 1855–86), 1:40.

SELECTING THE SALT LAKE TEMPLE SITE. If the inquiry is in the hearts of the people—"Does the Lord require the building of a temple at our hands?" I can say that He requires it just as much as ever He required one to be built elsewhere. If you should ask, "Brother Brigham, have you any knowledge concerning this? have you ever had a revelation from heaven upon it?" I can answer truly, it is before me all the time, not only to-day, but it was almost five years ago, when we were on this ground, looking for locations, sending our scouting parties through the country, to the right and to the left, to the north and the south, to the east and the west; before we had any returns from any of them, I knew, just as well as I now know, that this was the ground on which to erect a temple—it was before me.

The Lord wished us to gather to this place, He wished us to cultivate the earth, and make these valleys like the Garden of Eden, and make all the improvements in our power, and build a temple as soon as circumstances would permit. And further, if the people and the Lord required it, I would give a written revelation, but let the people do the things they know to be right.

—*14 February 1853*, Journal of Discourses, *1:277.*

THE PATTERN OF THE LORD'S EXPERIENCES. The Latter-day Saints in their trials, privations, and afflictions often wonder why it is they are called to pass through such heart rending scenes. . . .

The Lord Jehovah never operates by blessings, by favors, by judgment, or by any other one of His providences, beyond His own capacity, and that with which he is well acquainted, and has passed through and experienced Himself. If he has received his exaltation without being hungry, cold, and naked; without passing through sickness, pestilence, and distress, by the same rule we may expect to be exalted to the same crown, to the same glory and exaltation. But if he deals out to us afflictions, persecutions, pain, distress, famine, perplexity, bloodshed, driving, privations of every kind, it is the way that leads to the same exaltation He enjoys. No man who is well instructed in the things of God would exclaim: "The God I serve has received His exaltation without suffering, and learning by his faithfulness." If God has received his exaltation in this way, He cannot in right, and in justice, call upon us to earn it by suffering, for He would then require that of us He Himself was not subject to. . . .

Christ is our Elder Brother, and God is the Father of our Spirits, as well as of the spirit of our Lord Jesus Christ; He is God of the Savior, and He is our God; He is His father, and He is our father. And we are brethren and are all one in Christ, if we are His servants, and we shall be exalted to the same power, glory, and exaltation with our Elder Brother. . . .

From the first dawn of reason upon my infant brain to this hour, have I ever asked God to turn away affliction from me? I have always felt that I had faith to endure, and that He would sustain me. I have asked the Lord to uphold me in certain places and circumstances, and to give grace and the light of His spirit to enable me to endure faithful to Him, but I have never asked Him to remove the affliction; neither have I ever asked the Lord to screen this people from being driven from their homes, and inheritances, for I knew it was necessary they should be tried in all things, that they might obtain experience.

— "*God Has Experienced Everything,*" 1 *October 1854, Salt Lake City, in* Mormon Heritage 1 *(November 1985): 4–6.*

VISIONS, REVELATIONS, MIRACLES, AND TESTIMONY.

Men who have professedly seen the most, known and understood the most, in this Church, and who have testified in the presence of large congregations, in the name of Israel's God,

that they have seen Jesus, &c., have been the very men who
have left this kingdom, before others who had to live by faith.
I have a witness right before me, and I am fearful every time
that a man or woman comes to me and relates great visions,
saying, "I have had a vision, an angel came and told me thus
and so; the visions of eternity were opened, and I saw thus
and so; I saw my destiny; I saw what the brethren would do
with me; I foresaw this and that. Look out for that man or
woman going to the devil. . . .

So when individuals are blessed with visions, revelations,
and great manifestations, look out, then the devil is nigh you,
and you will be tempted in proportion to the vision, revelation,
or manifestation you have received. Hence thousands, when
they are off their guard, give way to the severe temptations
which come upon them, and behold they are gone.

You will recollect that I have often told you that miracles
would not save a person, and I say that they never should. If
I were to see a man come in here this day, and say, "I am
the great one whom the Lord has sent," and cause fire to come
down in our sight, through the ceiling that is over our heads,
I would not believe any more for that. It is no matter what
he does, I cannot believe any more on that account. What
will make me believe? What made the Twelve Apostles of
Jesus Christ witnesses? What constituted them Apostles—
special witnesses to the world? Was it seeing miracles? No.
What was it? The visions of their minds were opened, and it
was necessary that a few should receive light, knowledge, and
intelligence, that all the powers of earth and hell could not
gainsay or compete with. That witness was within them, and
yet, after all that was done for them, after all that Jesus showed
them, and after all the power of the spirit of revelation which
they possessed, you find that one of them apostatized, turned
away and sold his Lord and master for thirty pieces of silver,
in consequence of his not being firm to his covenant in the

hour of darkness and temptation. Another of them was ready to say, "I do not know anything about the Lord Jesus Christ," and denied him with cursing and swearing.

Some are apt now to say, "I don't know anything about this Mormonism, I don't know about the Priesthood." Did you not once know? "I thought I did." Did you not once know that Joseph Smith was a Prophet? "I thought I did." Did you not once know that this was the kingdom of God set up on the earth? "I thought I did, but now I find myself deceived." What is the reason? Because they give way to temptation; they may have had great light, knowledge, and understanding, the vision of their minds may have been opened and eternity exhibited to their view, but when this is closed up, in proportion to the light given to them, so is the darkness that comes upon them to try them. . . .

Again to the witness, that is on my mind. It was necessary for Jesus Christ to open the heavens to certain individuals that they might be witnesses of his personage, death, sufferings, and resurrection; those men were witnesses. But as Jesus appeared to the two brethren going out of Jerusalem, he was made known to them in the breaking of bread. Now suppose he had eaten that bread, and gone out without opening their eyes, how could they have known that he was the Savior who had been crucified on Mount Calvary? They could not; but in the breaking of bread the vision of their minds was opened. This was necessary in order to constitute safe witnesses, and they returned to Jerusalem and told the brethren what they had seen.

When Jesus came and ate fish broiled upon the coals, and told his disciples to cast the net on the other side of the ship, which they did and got it so full that they could hardly draw it to shore, would they have known that he was the Savior by the catching and hauling in a wonderful quantity of fish, or by anything else that they could have seen with their natural eyes? No, but when he came and ate the broiled fish and honeycomb, he opened their eyes and they saw that he was present with them. He had been back to his Father, had ascended to heaven and again descended, and opened their minds that they might be special witnesses. This is necessary. Did all the disciples, in the days of the Apostles, see the risen Jesus? No. Did all the disciples have visions? No, they did not. Do they now? No. I know the inquiry may arise, can a person be a real disciple without having visions? Yes, but that person cannot be a special witness to the doctrine he believes in.

What makes true disciples to a doctrine, to a religion, to a creed, or to a faith, no matter what it is which is subscribed to? To be faithful adherents to those articles of faith or doctrine taught, makes them true disciples to that religion or doctrine. Then if we have the religion of the Savior we are entitled to the blessings precisely as they were anciently. Not that all had visions, not that all had dreams, not that all had the gift of tongues or the interpretation of tongues, but every man received according to his capacity and the blessing of the Giver. "Well, brother Brigham, have you had visions?" Yes, I have. "Have you had revelations?" Yes, I have them all the time, I live constantly by the principle of revelation. I never received one iota of intelligence, from the letter A to what I now know, I mean that, from the very start of my life to this time, I have never received one particle of intelligence only by revelation, no matter whether father or mother revealed it, or my sister, or neighbor.

No person receives knowledge only upon the principle of revelation, that is, by having something revealed to them. "Do you have the revelations of the Lord Jesus Christ?" I will leave that for others to judge. If the Lord requires anything of this people, and speaks through me, I will tell them of it; but if He does not, still we all live by the principle of revelation.

Who reveals? Every body around us; we learn of each other. . . .

You may be tried and cast down, and be inclined to say that the Lord has not revealed this or that to you, but that has nothing to do with me or you. I do not desire to dictate the Lord in that matter; all I have to do is to concern myself with the things He requires of me, for it is His right to pursue His own way, and take His own time and course in dealing with me. Can you gain a victory? You can. . . .

I know what I am a witness of, and I know my Apostleship. I am a witness that Joseph Smith was a Prophet of God. What an uproar it would make in the Christian world to say, I am an Apostle of Joseph. Write it down, and write it back to your friends in the east, that I am an Apostle of Joseph Smith. He was a man of God and had the revelations of Jesus Christ, and the words of Jesus Christ to the people. He did build and establish the kingdom of God on earth, and through him the Lord Almighty again restored the Priesthood to the children of men.

Brethren, I am a witness of that; not by my laying hands on the sick and they being healed, nor by the revelations which are given of him in the Bible, but by receiving the same Spirit and witness which the ancients received; by the visions of the heavens being opened to my mind; by my understanding that which is revealed in the Book of Mormon, and that which Joseph revealed as comprised in the Book of Doctrine and Covenants.

I am a witness that those are the revelations of the Lord through Joseph Smith, in this the last dispensation for the gathering of the people; and all who reject my testimony will go to hell, so sure as there is one, no matter whether it be hot or cold; they will incur the displeasure of the Father and of the Son.

I am a witness of this; and all who will hear the voice of

the servants of God, pay attention to what they say, and obey the commandments given to the people, shall receive a testimony and know that we tell them the truth, that Joseph is a Prophet of God, and did actually finish the work which the Lord gave him to do, sealed his testimony with his blood, and has gone to dwell in the world of spirits, until he gets his body. All will have to acknowledge that this is true.

—17 February 1856, Journal of Discourses, 3:205–6, 208–9, 211–13.

THE DIFFERENCE BETWEEN CHRIST AND ANY OTHER MAN. All the difference between Jesus Christ and any other man that ever lived on the earth, from the days of Adam until now, is simply this, the Father, after He had once been in the flesh, and lived as we live, obtained His exaltation, attained to thrones, gained the ascendancy over principalities and powers, and had the knowledge and power to create—to bring forth and organize the elements upon natural principles. . . .

When the time came that His first-born, the Saviour, should come into the world and take a tabernacle, the Father came Himself and favoured that spirit with a tabernacle instead of letting any other man do it. The Saviour was begotten by the Father of His spirit, by the same Being who is the Father of our spirits, and that is all the organic difference between Jesus Christ and you and me . . . .

I know my heavenly Father and Jesus Christ whom He has sent, and this is eternal life.

—8 February 1857, Journal of Discourses, 4:217–18.

KEEP THE LORD'S CONFIDENCES. Should you receive a vision of revelation from the Almighty, one that the Lord gave you concerning yourselves, or this people, but which you are not to reveal on account of your not being the proper person, or because it ought not to be known by the people at present, you should shut it up and seal it as close, and lock it as tight as heaven is to you, and make it as secret as the grave. The Lord has no confidence in those who reveal secrets, for He cannot safely reveal Himself to such persons. It is as much as He can do to get a particle of sense into some of the best and most influential men in the Church, in regard to real confidence in themselves. They cannot keep things within their own bosoms.

. They are like a great many boys and men that I have seen, who would cause even a sixpence, when given to them, to become so hot that it would burn through the pocket of a new vest, or pair of pantaloons, if they could not spend it. It could not stay with them; they would feel so tied up because they were obliged to keep it, that the very fire of discontent would cause it to burn through the pocket, and they would lose the sixpence. This is the case with a great many of the Elders of Israel, with regard to keeping secrets. They burn with the idea, "O, I know things that brother Brigham does not understand." Bless your souls, I guess you do. Don't you think that there are some things that you do not understand? "There may be some things which I do not understand." That is as much as to say, "I know more than you." I am glad of it, if you do. I wish that you knew a dozen times more. When you see a person of that character, he has no soundness within him.

If a person understands God and godliness, the principles of heaven, the principle of integrity, and the Lord reveals anything to that individual, no matter what, unless He gives permission to disclose it, it is locked up in eternal silence. And when persons have proven to their messengers that their bosoms are like the lock-ups of eternity, then the Lord says, I can reveal anything to them, because they never will disclose it until I tell them to.

—15 March 1857, Journal of Discourses, 4:288.

KEEP CONFIDENCES, AND YOU WILL BE GIVEN MORE. You often hear people desiring more of the knowledge of God, more of the wisdom of God, more of the power of God. They want more revelation, to know more about the kingdom of heaven, in heaven and on the earth, and they wish to learn and increase.

There is one principle that I wish the people would understand and lay to heart. Just as fast as you will prove before your God that you are worthy to receive the mysteries, if you please to call them so, of the kingdom of heaven—that you are full of confidence in God—that you will never betray a thing that God tells you—that you will never reveal to your neighbour that which ought not to be revealed, as quick as you prepare to be entrusted with the things of God, there is an eternity of them to bestow upon you. Instead of pleading with the Lord to bestow more upon you, plead with yourselves to have confidence in yourselves, to have integrity in yourselves, and know when to speak and what to speak, what to reveal, and how to carry yourselves and walk before the Lord. And just as fast as you prove to Him that you will preserve everything secret that ought to be—that you will deal out to your neighbours all which you ought, and no more, and learn how to dispense your knowledge to your families, friends, neighbours, and brethren, the Lord will bestow upon you, and give to you, and bestow upon you, until finally he will say to you, "You shall never fall; your salvation is sealed unto you; you are sealed up unto eternal life and salvation, through your integrity."

—*28 June 1857,* Journal of Discourses, *4:371–72.*

WHEN HE COMES. Jesus has been upon the earth a great many more times than you are aware of. When Jesus makes his next appearance upon the earth, but few of this Church and kingdom will be prepared to receive him and see him face to face and converse with him; but he will come to his temple. Will he remain and dwell upon the earth a thousand years, without returning? He will come here, and return to his mansion where he dwells with his Father, and come again to the earth, and again return to his Father, according to my understanding. Then angels will come and begin to resurrect the dead, and the Saviour will also raise the dead, and they will receive the keys of the resurrection, and will begin to assist in that work. Will the wicked know of it? They will know just as much about that as they now know about "Mormonism," and no more.

When all nations are so subdued to Jesus that every knee shall bow and every tongue shall confess, there will still be millions on the earth who will not believe in him; but they will be obliged to acknowledge his kingly government.

—*22 May 1859*, Journal of Discourses, *7:142*.

OUR EVERLASTING FRIENDS. The Apostles and Prophets, when speaking of our relationship to God, say that we are flesh of his flesh and bone of his bone. God is our Father, and Jesus Christ is our Elder Brother, and both are our everlasting friends. This is Bible doctrine. Do you know the relationship you sustain to them? Christ has overcome; and now it is for us to overcome, that we may be crowned with him heirs of God—joint heirs with Christ.

—*19 June 1859*, Journal of Discourses, *6:332*.

PERHAPS THE LORD WILL APPEAR TO ME. I have flattered myself, if I am as faithful as I know how to be to my God, and my brethren, and to all my covenants, and faithful in the discharge of my duty, when I have lived to be as old as was Moses when the Lord appeared to him, that perhaps I then may hold communion with the Lord, as did Moses. I am not now in that position, though I know much more than I did twenty, ten, or five years ago. But have I yet lived to the state of perfection that I can commune in person with the Father and the Son at my will and pleasure? No, — though I hold myself in readiness that he can wield me at his will and pleasure. If I am faithful until I am eighty years of age, perhaps the Lord will appear to me and personally dictate me in the management of his Church and people. A little over twenty years, and if I am faithful, perhaps I will obtain that favour with my Father and God.

I am not to obtain this privilege at once or in a moment.
—*1 September 1859*, Journal of Discourses, *7:243.*

THE TESTIMONY OF JESUS IS THE PRIVILEGE OF ALL. It is the privilege of all to have the testimony of Jesus — to have the Spirit of prophecy. I have no greater privilege to enjoy the Spirit of prophecy than you have. I have no better right to the Holy Ghost than you. If you will live as you are taught, you will walk in darkness no more, but will walk in the light of life.
—*5 April 1860*, Journal of Discourses, *8:33.*

THE VOICE OF THE GOOD SHEPHERD. When the voice of the Good Shepherd is heard, the honest in heart believe and receive it. It is good to taste with the inward taste, to see with the inward eyes, and to enjoy with the sensations of the ever-living spirit. No person, unless he is an adulterer, a fornicator, covetous, or an idolater, will ever require a miracle; in other words, no good, honest person ever will.
—*8 April 1860*, Journal of Discourses, *8:42.*

TRUST THE TESTIMONY OF HIS FRIENDS. The Lord Jesus Christ might come among us and we would not know Him; and if he were to come in our midst and speak unto us to-day, we might suppose Him to be one of our returned missionaries; and if He was to make himself known unto us, some might say to Him, as it was said by one of old, "Lord, show us the Father, and it sufficeth us." He would simply say, "He that hath seen me hath seen the Father, and how sayest thou, then, shew us the Father?" It is written of Jesus, that, besides His being the brightness of His Father's glory, He is also "the express image of His person." The knowledge of the character of the Only Begotten of the Father comes to us through the testimony, not of disinterested witnesses, but of His friends, those who were most especially and deeply interested for their own welfare, and the welfare of their brethren. We have no testimony concerning the Savior's character and works, only from those who were thus interested in His welfare and success, and in the building up of His kingdom. It has been often said, if a disinterested witness would testify that Joseph Smith is a prophet of God, many might believe his testimony; but no person could be believed, by any intelligent person, who would testify to a matter of such importance, and who would still view it as a thing in which he had no interest. But they who are interested, who know the worth of that man and understand the spirit and the power of his mission, and the character of the Being that sent and ordained him, are the proper persons to testify of the truth of his mission, and they are the most interested of any living upon the earth. So it was with those who bore witness of the Savior, and of His mission on the earth. . . .

As to whether the Savior has got a body or not is no question with those who possess the gift and power of the Holy Ghost, and are endowed with the Holy Priesthood; they know that he was a man in the flesh, and is now a man in the heavens; He was a man subject to sin, to temptation, and to weaknesses; but He is now a man that is above all this—a man in perfection. . . .

We have not seen the person of the Father, neither have

we seen that of the Son; but we have seen the children of the Father, and the brethren of the Savior, who are in every way like them in physical appearance and organization.

    −8 *January 1865,* Journal of Discourses, *11:41–42.*

THE PROPHET RECEIVES REVELATION FROM THE LORD. I can call to mind revelations which the Lord delivered to His servant Joseph, that when they were written and given to the people there would not be one in fifty of the members of the Church who could say that they knew, by the revelations of the Lord Jesus, that they were of the Lord; but they would have to pray and exercise faith to be able to receive them, and in some instances some apostatized in consequence of revelations that had been given. This was the case when the "Vision" was given through Joseph Smith and Sidney Rigdon.

    At that time there was not as many in the whole Church as there is in this congregation. Yes, many forsook the faith when the Lord revealed the fact to Joseph Smith and Sidney Rigdon, as He did to His ancient Apostles, that all would receive a salvation except those who had sinned a sin unto death, of which the Apostle John said—"I do not say that ye shall pray for it." I prayed and reflected about it, and so did others. I became satisfied that, when a revelation came to Joseph for the people to perform any labor or duty, it was their privilege to go to with their might and do it collectively and individually, not waiting for the manifestations of the Spirit to me, but believing that the Prophet knew more than I knew, that the Lord spoke through him, and that He could do as He pleased about speaking to me. This is a close point; but I will tell you what is right, what is the duty of the Latter-day Saints, unless they can, by undeniable proof, show that the word of the Lord has not come through the President, they have no right to hesitate one moment in performing the duties required of them. This is the way I understand revelation.

    —*3 November 1867,* Journal of Discourses, *12:104–5.*

KEEP MY COMMANDMENTS. Jesus says, pointedly, "If ye love me, keep my commandments." This is the test? Are there any commandments? Yes, plenty of them, and the only way to prove our belief in and love for the Lord Jesus is by observing the sayings that he has left on record.

    —*24 April 1870,* Journal of Discourses, *13:331.*

DON'T WAIT FOR THE LORD TO EXPRESS HIS LOVE. Do I wish to wait until the Lord speaks from heaven to me? No, the Lord has planted within me knowledge and wisdom to distinguish between right and wrong, and if I wait until his voice comes from heaven to tell me that I am a sinner, or until he gives me some particular manifestation of approval on my attempting to forsake evil, I may wait a great while. . . . I do not care if I live my whole lifetime without a testimony from the Lord; not that he leaves his children thus; he has never been so hard-hearted, so austere a master as to leave one of his children with full purpose of heart to serve him and do his will without a witness of his approval. But, suppose he were disposed to do so, I am under obligations, on the principles of right and wrong, to forsake evil, and to plant within me every principle of purity and holiness, whether or not the Lord manifest unto me that I am his son and that he is pleased with me. . . .

    I am under obligation to take a course which will sustain life within myself and others, on rational principles, without any special manifestation from God. I do not know that I shall inquire of the Lord whether he loves me or not. I do not know that I have ever taken pains to ask him. I have professed religion somewhere near fifty years, and I do not know that

I ever asked the Lord whether he loved me or not. I want to take a course that I can love purity and holiness. If I do this, then I love the Lord and keep his commandments, and that is enough for me. If he is not disposed to like me as well as he did John, "the beloved disciple," who leaned upon his breast on a certain occasion, and tells me to sit yonder instead of here, it is all right, I am as satisfied to sit there as here. I want to preserve my identity and to increase in intelligence, and if I can do this I do not know that I care, particularly, with regard to how much, in weight or measure, the Lord loves me or does not love me. There is one fact that I do know, he will love me all he should.

—*7 May 1871, Journal of Discourses, 14:110–12, 114.*

THE SPIRIT OF GOD CANNOT BE DECEIVED. I know that there are such cities as London, Paris, and New York— from my own experience or from that of others; I know that the sun shines, I know that I exist and have a being, and I testify that there is a God, and that Jesus Christ lives, and that he is the Savior of the world. Have you been to heaven and learned to the contrary? I know that Joseph Smith was a Prophet of God, and that he had many revelations. Who can disprove this testimony? Any one may dispute it, but there is no one in the world who can disprove it. I have had many revelations; I have seen and heard for myself, and know these things are true, and nobody on earth can disprove them. The eye, the ear, the hand, all the senses may be deceived, but the Spirit of God cannot be deceived; and when inspired with that Spirit, the whole man is filled with knowledge, he can see with a spiritual eye, and he knows that which is beyond the power of man to controvert. What I know concerning God, concerning the earth, concerning government, I have received from the heavens, not alone through my natural ability, and I give God the glory and the praise. Men talk about what has been accomplished under my direction, and attribute it to my wisdom and ability; but it is all by the power of God, and by intelligence received from him.

— *18 May 1873*, Journal of Discourses, *16:46.*

EARLY MANIFESTATIONS. While we were in England, I think, the Lord manifested to me by visions and his Spirit, things that I did not then understand. I never opened my mouth to any person concerning them, until I returned to Nauvoo. Joseph had never mentioned this, there had never been a thought of it in the Church that I knew anything about at that time. But I had this for myself, and I kept it to myself, and when I returned home and Joseph revealed these things to me, I then understood the reflections that were upon my mind while in England. But this was not until after I had told him what I understood. I saw that he was after something by his conversation, leading my mind along, and others, to see how we could bear this. This was in 1841; the revelation was given in 1843, but the doctrine was revealed before this; and when I told Joseph what I understood, which was right in front of my house in the street, as he was shaking hands and leaving me, he turned round and looked me in the eyes, and says he — "Brother Brigham, are you speaking what you understand, — are you in earnest?" Says I — "I speak just as the Spirit manifests to me." Says he — "God bless you, the Lord has opened your mind," and he turned and went off.

— *23 June 1874*, Journal of Discourses, *18:241.*

Chapter 3

JOHN TAYLOR

Born: 1 November 1808
Ordained an Apostle: 19 December 1838
Sustained as President: 10 October 1880
Died: 25 July 1887

PRINCIPLES AS FIRM AS JEHOVAH'S THRONE. The idea of the church being disorganized and broken up because of the Prophet and Patriarch being slain, is preposterous. This church has the seeds of immortality in its midst. It is not of man, nor by man—it is the offspring of Deity: it is organized after the pattern of heavenly things, through the principles of revelation; by the opening of the heavens, by the ministering of angels, and the revelations of Jehovah. It is not affected by the death of one or two, or fifty individuals; it possesses a priesthood after the order of Melchisedec, having the power of an endless life, "without beginning of days, or end of years." It is organized for the purpose of saving this generation, and generations that are past; it exists in time and will exist in eternity. This church fail? No! Times and seasons may change, revolution may succeed revolution, thrones may be cast down, and empires be dissolved, earthquakes may rend the earth from centre to circumference, the mountains may be hurled out of their places, and the mighty ocean be moved from its bed; but amidst the crash of worlds and crack of matter, truth, eternal truth, must remain unchanged, and those principles which God has revealed to his Saints be unscathed amidst the warring elements, and remain as firm as the throne of Jehovah.

—Times and Seasons, 15 December 1844, p. 744.

CHRIST IS OUR LIFE. I don't believe in meeting Christ at death. I believe that Christ is our life and that when he who is our life shall appear, we shall appear like unto him in glory, he is our life, our living head, and by the power that dwells in him, we may be raised to immortal bloom, and grasp eternity itself. . . . We can look unto Jesus Christ, forever. We can do the works that he did, and greater; because he has gone to the Father, for we are told, all things were created by him, and for him; principalities, powers, things present, and things to come; and if ever we should get to such a state, as to be like him we might be able to do such kind of business as he did; . . . Jesus was not prepared to govern, till he was placed in circumstances that gave him experience. The scriptures say, it is necessary to the bringing of many souls to glory, that the Captain of our salvation should be made perfect [through] sufferings. So, he was not perfect before, but he had to come here to be made perfect; he had to come here to pass through a multitude of sufferings, and be tempted and tried in all points like unto us, because it was necessary. Had it not been necessary he would not have been placed in those circumstances, and this is the reason why we are here, and kicked and cuffed round, and hated and despised, by the world. The reason why we do not live in peace is because we are not prepared for it. We are tempted and tried, driven, mobbed, and robbed; apostates are in our midst, which cause trouble and vexation of spirit, and it is all to keep down our pride and learn us to honor the God of Jacob in all things and to make us appear what we really are.

—Times and Seasons, *20 January 1846, p. 1100.*

TEMPTED IN ALL THINGS. It is necessary, then, that we pass through the school of suffering, trial, affliction, and privation, to know ourselves, to know others, and to know our God. Therefore it was necessary, when the Saviour was upon the earth, that he should be tempted in all points, like unto us, and "be touched with the feeling of our infirmities," to comprehend the weaknesses and strength, the perfections and imperfections of poor fallen human nature. And having accomplished the thing he came into the world to do; having had to grapple with the hypocrisy, corruption, weakness, and imbecility of man; having met with temptation and trial in all its various forms, and overcome, he has become a "faithful High Priest" to intercede for us in the everlasting kingdom of His Father. He knows how to estimate and put a proper value upon human nature, for he having been placed in the same position as we are, knows how to bear with our weaknesses and infirmities, and can fully comprehend the depth, power, and strength of the afflictions and trials that men have to cope with in this world, and thus understandingly and by experience, he can bear with them as a father and an elder brother.

It is necessary, also, inasmuch as we profess that we are aiming at the same glory, exaltation, power, and blessings in the eternal world, that we should pass through the same afflictions, endure the same privations, conquer as he conquered, and overcome as he did, and thus by integrity, truth, virtue, purity, and a high-minded and honorable course before God, angels, and men, secure for ourselves an eternal exaltation in the eternal world, as he did.

— *12 June 1853*, Journal of Discourses, *1:148–49.*

PRAISE THE LORD. Who made this earth? The Lord.

Who sustains it? The Lord.

Who feeds and clothes the millions of the human family that exist upon it, both Saint and sinner? The Lord.

Who upholds everything in the universe? The Lord.

Who provides for the myriads of cattle, fish, and fowl that inhabit the sea, earth, and air? The Lord.

Who has implanted in them that instinct which causes them to take care of their young, and that power by which to propagate their species? The Lord.

Who has given to man understanding? The Lord.

Who has given to the Gentile philosopher, machinist, &c., every particle of intelligence they have with regard to the electric telegraph, the power and application of steam to the wants of the human family, and every kind of invention that has been brought to light during the last century? The Lord.

Who sets up the kings, emperors, and potentates that rule and govern the universe? The Lord.

And who is there that acknowledges his hand? Where is the nation, the people, the church even, or other power that does it? You may wander east, west, north, and south, and you cannot find it in any church or government on the earth, except the Church of Jesus Christ of Latter-day Saints.

— *1 November 1857*, Journal of Discourses, *6:24.*

I KNOW AS JOB KNEW. I want a part in the resurrection. The angel said, "Blessed and holy is he who has part in the first resurrection." I want to have part in the first resurrection. It is that which leads me to hope. It is that hope which buoys me up under difficulties and sustains me while passing through tribulation, for I know as well as Job knew that my "Redeemer lives, and that He shall stand in the latter day upon the earth," and I know that I shall stand upon it with him. I therefore bear this testimony.

    —6 May 1870, Journal of Discourses, 13:231.

GOD'S REVELATIONS NOW AS COMPARED TO OTHER DAYS.

I have heard some people say—"If God revealed himself to men in other days, why not reveal himself to us?" I say, why not, indeed, to us? Why should not men in this day be put in possession of the same light, truth and intelligence, and the same means of acquiring a knowledge of God as men in other ages and eras have enjoyed? Why should they not? Who can answer the question? Who can solve the problem? Who can tell why these things should not exist to-day, as much as in any other day? If God is God and men are men, if God has a design in relation to the earth on which we live, and in relation to the eternities that are to come; if men have had a knowledge of God in days past, why not in this day? What good reason is there why it should not be so? Say some— "Oh, we are so enlightened and intelligent now. In former ages, when the people were degraded and in darkness, it was necessary that he should communicate intelligence to the human family; but we live in the blaze of Gospel day, in an age of light and intelligence." Perhaps we do; I rather doubt it. I have a great many misgivings about the intelligence that men boast so much of in this enlightened day. There were men in those dark ages who could commune with God, and who, by the power of faith, could draw aside the curtain of eternity and gaze upon the invisible world. There were men who could tell the destiny of the human family, and the events which would transpire throughout every subsequent period of time until the final winding-up scene. There were men who could gaze upon the face of God, have the ministering of angels, and unfold the future destinies of the world. If those were dark ages I pray God to give me a little darkness, and deliver me from the light and intelligence that prevail in our day; for as a rational, intelligent, immortal being who has to do with time and eternity, I consider it one of the greatest acquirements for men to become acquainted with their God and with their future destiny. . . .

Life and immortality, we are told, were brought to light by the Gospel. And how is that? Why, it is a very simple thing, a very simple thing indeed. When Jesus was upon the earth he, we are told, came to introduce the Gospel. He appeared on this continent as on the continent of Asia for that purpose; and in so doing he made known unto men certain principles pertaining to their being and origin, and their relationship to God; pertaining to the earth on which we live, and to the heavens with which we expect to be associated; pertaining to the beings who have existed and those who will exist; pertaining to the resurrection of the dead and the life and glory of the world to come. This is what the Gospel unfolds.

—7 September 1873, Journal of Discourses, 16:197–98.

REVELATION ONLY AS THE LORD PERMITS. No man can reveal anything pertaining to these matters only as it is given to him, and he is permitted by the Lord, who is the Author of all light, intelligence and knowledge which we, his children, possess. And he has gathered us together for the purpose of instructing us that we may operate with him and by him and through the intelligence which he imparts, in building up his Zion of the last days.

—1 December 1878, Journal of Discourses, 20:133–34.

I LEARN THE WILL OF GOD AND THEN DO IT. I know,

furthermore, that as President of this Church I should not know how to dictate if the Lord did not help me. Should I desire people to yield to my ideas? I have no ideas only as God gives them to me; neither should you. Some people are very persistent in having their own way and carrying out their own peculiar theories. I have no thoughts of that kind, but I have a desire, when anything comes along, to learn the will of God, and then to do it, and to teach my brethren to do it, that we may all grow up unto Christ our living head, that we may be acquainted with correct principles and govern ourselves accordingly.

   — 19 October 1881, Journal of Discourses, 22:314.

HEAR HIM. In the commencement of the work, the Father and the Son appeared to Joseph Smith. And when they appeared to him, the Father, pointing to the Son, said, "This is my beloved Son, hear him." As much as to say, "I have not come to teach and instruct you; but I refer you to my Only Begotten, who is the Mediator of the New Covenant, the Lamb slain from before the foundation of the world; I refer you to Him as your Redeemer, your High Priest and Teacher. Hear Him."

   — 20 October 1881, Journal of Discourses, 26:106.

GATHERED THROUGH THE ATONEMENT. God, our heavenly Father, has gathered unto himself, through the atonement of Jesus Christ, very many great and honorable men who have lived upon the earth, and who have been clothed with the powers of the Priesthood. Those men having held that Priesthood and administered in it upon the earth are now in the heavens operating with the Priesthood in the heavens in connection with the Priesthood that exists now upon the earth.

   — 24 July 1882, Journal of Discourses, 23:176.

INFINITE ATONEMENT. We are told in . . . the Book of Mormon [2 Nephi 9] that the atonement must needs be infinite. Why did it need an infinite atonement? For the simple reason that a stream can never rise higher than its fountain; and man having assumed a fleshly body and become of the earth earthy, and through the violation of a law having cut himself off from his association with his Father, and become subject to death; in this condition, as the mortal life of man was short, and in and of himself he could have no hope of benefitting himself, or redeeming himself from his fallen condition, or of bringing himself back to the presence of his Father, some superior agency was needed to elevate him above his low and degraded position. This superior agency was the Son of God, who had not, as man had, violated a law of His Father, but was yet one with His Father, possessing His glory, His power, His authority, His dominion.

—Mediation and Atonement of Our Lord and Savior Jesus Christ (*Salt Lake City: Deseret News Company, 1882; 1975 reprint*), 145.

THE GLORY BE THINE. It is consistent to believe that at this Council in the heavens the plan that should be adopted in relation to the sons of God who were then spirits, and had not yet obtained tabernacles, was duly considered. For, in view of the creation of the world and the placing of men upon it, whereby it would be possible for them to obtain tabernacles, and in those tabernacles obey laws of life, and with them again be exalted among the Gods, we are told, that at that time, "the morning stars sang together, and all the sons of God shouted for joy." The question then arose, how, and upon what principle, should the salvation, exaltation and eternal glory of God's sons be brought about? It is evident that at that Council certain plans had been proposed and discussed, and that after a full discussion of those principles, and the declaration of the Father's will pertaining to His design, Lucifer

came before the Father, with a plan of his own, saying, "Behold
I, send me, I will be thy Son, and I will redeem all mankind,
that one soul shall not be lost, and surely I will do it; wherefore,
give me thine honor." But Jesus, on hearing this statement
made by Lucifer, said, "Father, thy will be done, and the glory
be thine forever." From these remarks made by the well beloved Son, we should naturally infer that in the discussion of
this subject the Father had made known His will and developed
His plan and design pertaining to these matters, and all that
His well beloved Son wanted to do was to carry out the will
of His Father, as it would appear had been before expressed.
He also wished the glory to be given to His Father, who, as
God the Father, and the originator and designer of the plan,
had a right to all the honor and glory. But Lucifer wanted to
introduce a plan contrary to the will of his Father, and then
wanted His honor, and said: "I will save every soul of man,
wherefore give me thine honor." He wanted to go contrary
to the will of his Father, and presumptuously sought to deprive
man of his free agency, thus making him a serf, and placing
him in a position in which it was impossible for him to obtain
that exaltation which God designed should be man's, through
obedience to the law which He had suggested; and again,
Lucifer wanted the honor and power of his Father, to enable
him to carry out principles which were contrary to the Father's
wish.

—Mediation and Atonement, 93–94.

THE AUTHOR OF ETERNAL LIFE AND EXALTATION.
Through the great atonement, the expiatory sacrifice of the
Son of God, it is made possible that man can be redeemed,
restored, resurrected and exalted to the elevated position designed for him in the creation as a Son of God: that eternal
justice and law required the penalty to be paid by man himself,
or by the atonement of the Son of God: that Jesus offered

Himself as the great expiatory sacrifice; that this offering being in accordance with the demands or requirements of the law, was accepted by the great Lawgiver; that it was prefigured by sacrifices, and ultimately fulfilled by Himself according to the eternal covenant. . . .

The Savior thus becomes master of the situation—the debt is paid, the redemption made, the covenant fulfilled, justice satisfied, the will of God done, and all power is now given into the hands of the Son of God—the power of the resurrection, the power of the redemption, the power of salvation, the power to enact laws for the carrying out and accomplishment of this design. Hence life and immortality are brought to light, the Gospel is introduced, and He becomes the author of eternal life and exaltation, He is the Redeemer, the Resurrector, the Savior of man and the world; and He has appointed the law of the Gospel as the medium which must be complied with in this world or the next, as He complied with His Father's law; hence "he that believeth shall be saved, and he that believeth not shall be damned."

The plan, the arrangement, the agreement, the covenant was made, entered into and accepted before the foundation of the world; it was prefigured by sacrifices, and was carried out and consummated on the cross.

Hence being the mediator between God and man, He becomes by right the dictator and director on earth and in heaven for the living and for the dead, for the past, the present and the future, pertaining to man as associated with this earth or the heavens, in time or eternity, the Captain of our salvation, the Apostle and High-Priest of our profession, the Lord and Giver of life.

—*Mediation and Atonement, 170–71.*

ALL THAT HE IS. It may here be asked, What difference is there between the Son of God, as the Son of God, the

Redeemer, and those who believe in Him and partake of the blessings of the Gospel?

One thing, as we read, is that the Father gave Him power to have life in Himself: "For as the Father hath life in himself, so hath he given to the Son to have life in himself;" and further, He had power, when all mankind had lost their life, to restore life to them again; and hence He is the Resurrection and the Life, which power no other man possesses.

Another distinction is, that having this life in Himself, He had power, as He said, to lay down His life and to take it up again, which power was also given Him by the Father. This is also a power which no other being associated with this earth possesses.

Again, He is the brightness of His Father's glory and the express image of His person. Also, He doeth what He seeth the Father do, while we only do that which we are permitted and empowered to do by Him.

He is the Elect, the Chosen, and one of the Presidency in the heavens, and in Him dwells all the fulness of the Godhead bodily, which could not be said of us in any of these particulars.

Another thing is, that all power is given to Him in heaven and upon earth, which no earthly being could say.

It is also stated that Lucifer was before Adam; so was Jesus. And Adam, as well as all other believers, was commanded to do all that he did in the name of the Son, and to call upon God in His name for ever more; which honor was not applicable to any earthly being.

He, in the nearness of His relationship to the Father, seems to occupy a position that no other person occupies. He is spoken of as His well beloved Son, as the Only Begotten of the Father—does not this mean the only begotten after the flesh? If He was the first born and obedient to the laws of His Father, did He not inherit the position by right to be the representative of God, the Savior and Redeemer of the world? And was it not His peculiar right and privilege as the firstborn, the legitimate heir of God, the Eternal Father, to step forth, accomplish and carry out the designs of His Heavenly Father pertaining to the redemption, salvation, and exaltation of man? And being Himself without sin (which no other mortal was), He took the position of Savior and Redeemer, which by right belonged to Him as the first born. And does it not seem that in having a body specially prepared, and being the offspring of God, both in body and spirit, He stood pre-eminently in the position of the Son of God, or in the place of God, and was God, and was thus the fit and only Personage capable of making an infinite atonement? . . .

Though others might be the sons of God through Him, yet it needed His body, His fulfilment of the law, the sacrifice or offering up of that body in the atonement, before any of these others, who were also sons of God by birth in the spirit world, could attain to the position of sons of God as He was; and that only through His mediation and atonement. So that in Him, and of Him, and through Him, through the principle of adoption, could we alone obtain that position which is spoken of by John: "Beloved, now are we the sons of God; and it doth not yet appear what we shall be: but we know that when he shall appear we shall be like him, for we shall see him as he is." Thus His atonement made it possible for us to obtain exaltation, which we could not have possessed without it.

"His name shall be called Immanuel," which being interpreted is, God with us. Hence He is not only called the Son of God, the First Begotten of the Father, the Well Beloved, the Head, and Ruler, and Dictator of all things, Jehovah, the I Am, the Alpha and Omega, but He is also called the Very Eternal Father. Does not this mean that in Him were the attributes and power of the Very Eternal Father? For the angel

to Adam said that all things should be done in His
name. . . . "Wherefore, thou shalt do all that thou doest in
the name of the Son. And thou shalt repent, and shalt call
upon God, in the name of the Son, for evermore."
—*Mediation and Atonement, 135–38.*

BENEFITS OF THE RESURRECTION AND ATONEMENT.
The penalty of the broken law in Adam's day was death; and
death is passed upon all. The word of the Lord was, "In the
day that thou eatest thereof thou shalt surely die." The atonement made by Jesus Christ brought about the resurrection
from the dead, and restored life. And hence Jesus said: "I am
the Resurrection and the Life; he that believeth in me, though
he were dead, yet shall he live;" and Jesus Himself became
the first fruits of those who slept.

The next question that arises is, how far does this principle
extend and to whom is it applicable? It extends to all the
human family; to all men of every nation: as it is written:

"For, if by one man's offence death reigneth by one; much
more they which receive abundance of grace, and of the gift
of righteousness, shall reign in life by one, Jesus Christ. Therefore, as by the offence of one judgment came upon all men
to condemnation, even so by the righteousness of one the free
gift came upon all men unto justification of life."—Romans,
v, 17, 18.

This will not all take place at once. "But every man in
his own order: Christ, the first fruits; afterward they that are
Christ's at his coming."—1 Cor., xv, 23. "But the rest of the
dead lived not again until the thousand years were finished."—
Rev., xx, 5.

Hence what was lost in Adam was restored in Jesus Christ,
so far as all men are concerned in all ages, with some very
slight exceptions arising from an abuse of privileges. Transgression of the law brought death upon all the posterity of Adam,

the restoration through the atonement restored all the human family to life. "For since by man came death, by man came also the resurrection of the dead. For as in Adam all die, even so in Christ shall all be made alive." So that whatever was lost by Adam, was restored by Jesus Christ. . . .

This is one part of the restoration. This is the restoration of the body. The next question for us to examine is, How, and in what manner are men benefitted by the atonement and by the resurrection? In this, that the atonement having restored man to his former position before the Lord, it has placed him in a position and made it possible for him to obtain that exaltation and glory which it would have been impossible for him to have received without it; even to become a son of God by adoption; and being a son then an heir of God, and a joint heir with Jesus Christ; and that, as Christ overcame, He has made it possible, and has placed it within the power of believers in Him, also to overcome; and as He is authorized to inherit His Father's glory which He had with Him before the world was, with His resurrected body, so through the adoption, may we overcome and sit down with Him upon His throne, as He has overcome and has sat down upon His Father's throne. And as he has said, "I and the Father are one," so are the obedient saints one with Him, as He is one with the Father.

—Mediation and Atonement, 178–79.

I Will Be Your God. And I will bless and be with you, saith the Lord, and ye shall gather together in your holy places wherein ye assemble to call upon me, and ye shall ask for such things as are right, and I will hear your prayers, and my Spirit and power shall be with you, and my blessing shall rest upon you, upon your families, your dwellings and your households, upon your flocks and herds and fields, your orchards and vineyards, and upon all that pertains to you; and you shall be my people and I will be your God; and your enemies shall not have dominion over you, for I will preserve you and confound them, saith the Lord, and they shall not have power nor dominion over you; for my word shall go forth, and my work shall be accomplished, and my Zion shall be established, and my rule and my power and my dominion shall prevail among my people, and all nations shall yet acknowledge me.

—*Revelation given through President John Taylor, 13 October 1882, in B. H. Roberts,* The Life of John Taylor *(Salt Lake City: Bookcraft, 1963), 351.*

WALK IN THE FOOTSTEPS OF JESUS. I am kept busy every day with the duties of my office, just the same as when at home, surrounded with the endearments of family. These experiences, however, are necessary for us, if we would play the role of saints, as it has been, and is for others, who have walked in the footsteps of Jesus in the former ages. Jesus said when on the earth, battling with the same corrupt influences, "Blessed are ye when men shall revile you, and persecute you, and say all manner of evil against you falsely for my sake. Rejoice and be exceeding glad, for great is your reward in heaven, *for so persecuted they the prophets which were before you.*" This is a singular annunciation. Is it true? Yes, it was true in the prophets' days, it was true in the days of Jesus, it is true in our day. Shall we mourn and lament then over our little difficulties? No! A thousand times, No! But we will lift up our hearts and rejoice.

—*Letter to Maggie Taylor, 2 February 1887, Church Archives. Spelling and punctuation have been standardized.*

Chapter 4

WILFORD WOODRUFF

Born: 1 March 1807
Ordained an Apostle: 26 April 1839
Sustained as President: 7 April 1889
Died: 2 September 1898

PREPARED FOR THE COMING OF THE BRIDEGROOM.
If we are afraid to rebuke iniquity, or ashamed to cast if off ourselves, Israel would go to hell, we should be cut off as a people, and the Lord would raise up another; for He is bound to have a people in the last days who will keep His commandments, and magnify their calling, and prove themselves friends of God, and maintain the principles of righteousness, and honor them before God, angels, and men, that His kingdom may be established in purity, and be prepared for the coming of the Messiah; for Christ is coming again to earth; he is preparing the bride, and here is a portion of it before me to-day.

Will he receive us to himself? Are we prepared for his coming and kingdom and the fulness thereof, unless we are sanctified, and lay aside sin, and do right? No. We must sanctify ourselves, and keep the commandments of God, and do those things that are required at our hands, before we can be prepared for the coming of the Great Bridegroom.

—25 *February 1855*, Journal of Discourses, 2:202.

THE LORD CALLED ME ON A MISSION. In the fall I had a desire to go and preach the gospel. I knew the gospel which the Lord had revealed to Joseph Smith was true, and of such great value that I wanted to tell it to the people who had not heard it. It was so good and plain, it seemed to me I could make people believe it.

I was but a Teacher, and it is not a Teacher's office to go abroad and preach. I dared not tell any of the authorities of the Church that I wanted to preach, lest they might think I was seeking for an office.

I went into the woods where no one could see me, and I prayed to the Lord to open my way so that I could go and preach the gospel. While I was praying the Spirit of the Lord came upon me, and told me my prayer was heard and that my request should be granted.

I felt very happy, and got up and walked out of the woods into the traveled road, and there I met a High Priest who had lived in the same house with me some six months.

He had not said a word to me about preaching the gospel; but now, as soon as I met him, he said, "The Lord has revealed to me that it is your privilege to be ordained, and to go and preach the gospel."

I told him I was willing to do whatever the Lord required of me. I did not tell him I had just asked the Lord to let me go and preach.

In a few days a council was called at Lyman Wight's, and

I was ordained a Priest and sent on a mission into Arkansas and Tennessee.

—Leaves from My Journal, 4th ed. (Salt Lake City: Deseret News, 1909), 8–9.

THE LORD WARNS MANKIND. Do I delight in the destruction of the children of men? No. Does the Lord? No. He gives them timely warning, and if they do not listen to His counsel, they must suffer the consequences. He has determined, in the last days, in spite of earth and hell, wicked men, and devils, to establish His kingdom upon the earth; He has proclaimed it in the Bible, that it shall not be thrown down any more for ever. . . .

The Lord made the earth, and placed man upon it, and He owns it still, and He will cut off wickedness, no matter where it exists, so that there will be room for the good fruit to grow. As true as the Lord lives, if we wish to exist upon the earth in these days, we must be righteous; if we expect to have a place, an inheritance, and dwell on the earth, we must keep the law of God, or we shall be cut off. This will apply to all, to Jew and Gentile, bond and free; this will apply to all men in every nation, and under all circumstances.

25 February 1855, Journal of Discourses, 2:201.

JEWS WILL ACCEPT CHRIST WHEN HE COMES. Here is Judah, which is the tribe of Israel, from whom Jesus sprang; how many times have I seen them among the nations of the earth, standing in their synagogues, even grey-haired rabbis, with their faces to the east, calling on the great Eloheim to open the door for them to go back to Jerusalem, the land of their fathers, and to send their shiloh, their king of deliverance. When I have seen this my soul has been filled with a desire to proclaim unto them the word of God unto eternal life, but I knew I could not do this, the time had not come,

I could not preach to them. I might have stood in their midst for a month and preached unto them Jesus Christ or their shiloh and king, but I should have failed to establish one particle of faith in their minds that he was the true Messiah.

They do not believe in Jesus Christ; there is unbelief resting upon them, and will until they go home and rebuild Jerusalem and their temple more glorious than at the beginning, and then by and by, after this Church and kingdom has arisen up in its glory, the Saviour will come to them and show the wounds in his hands and side, and they will say to him, "Where did you get those wounds?" and he will answer, "In the house of my friends," and then their eyes will begin to open, and they will repent and mourn, they and their wives apart, and there will be a fountain opened for uncleanness to the house of Judah, and they will for the first time receive Jesus Christ as their Saviour, they will begin to comprehend where they have been wandering for the space of two thousand years.

—*22 February 1857*, Journal of Discourses, 4:232.

SIGNS OF THE SECOND COMING. No man knows the day or the hour when Christ will come, yet the generation has been pointed out by Jesus himself. He told his disciples when they passed by the temple as they walked out of Jerusalem that that generation should not pass away before not one stone of that magnificent temple should be left standing upon another and the Jews should be scattered among the nations; and history tells how remarkably that prediction was fulfilled. Moses and the prophets also prophesied of this as well as Jesus. The Savior, when speaking to his disciples of his second coming and the establishment of his kingdom on the earth, said the Jews should be scattered and trodden under foot until the times of the Gentiles were fulfilled. But, said he, when you see light breaking forth among the Gentiles, referring to the preaching of his Gospel amongst them; when you see salvation offered to the Gentiles, and the Jews — the seed of Israel — passed by, the last first and the first last; when you see this you may know that the time of my second coming is at hand as surely as you know that summer is nigh when the fig tree puts forth its leaves; and when these things commence that generation shall not pass away until all are fulfilled.

— 1 January 1871, Journal of Discourses, 14:5.

THE JEWS AND THE RIGHTEOUS WILL SEE SHILOH. The Jews have got to gather to their own land in unbelief. They will go and rebuild Jerusalem and their temple. They will take their gold and silver from the nations and will gather to the Holy Land, and when they have done this and rebuilt their city, the Gentiles, in fulfillment of the words of Ezekiel, Jeremiah and other prophets, will go up against Jerusalem to battle and to take a spoil and a prey; and then when they have taken one-half of Jerusalem captive and distressed the Jews for the last time on the earth, their Great Deliverer, Shiloh, will come. They do not believe in Jesus of Nazareth now, nor ever will until he comes and sets his foot on Mount Olivet and it cleaves in twain, one part going towards the east, and the other towards the west. Then, when they behold the wounds in his hands and in his feet, they will say, "Where did you get them?" And he will reply, "I am Jesus of Nazareth, King of the Jews, your Shiloh, him whom you crucified." Then, for the first time will the eyes of Judah be opened. They will remain in unbelief until that day. This is one of the events that will transpire in the latter day.

The Gospel of Christ has to go to the Gentiles until the Lord says "enough," until their times are fulfilled, and it will be in this generation. . . . We are living in a late age, although it is true there are a great many vast and important events to transpire in these days. But one thing is certain, though the Lord has not revealed the day nor the hour wherein the Son of Man shall come, he has pointed out the generation, and the signs predicted as the fore-runners of that great event have begun to appear in the heavens and on the earth, and they will continue until all is consummated. . . .

Who is going to be prepared for the coming of the Messiah? These men who enjoy the Holy Ghost and live under the inspiration of the Almighty, who abide in Jesus Christ and bring forth fruit to the honor and glory of God. No other people will be.

—*12 January 1873*, Journal of Discourses, *15:277–79*.

THE TESTIMONY OF THE HOLY GHOST. What is the greatest testimony any man or woman can have as to this being the work of God? I will tell you what is the greatest testimony I have ever had, the most sure testimony, that is the testimony of the Holy Ghost, the testimony of the Father and the Son. We may have the ministration of angels; we may be wrapt in the visions of heaven—these things as testimonies are very good, but when you receive the Holy Ghost, when you receive the testimony of the Father and the Son, it is a true principle to every man on earth, it deceives no man, and by that principle you can learn and understand the mind of God. Revelation has been looked upon by this Church, as well as by the world, as something very marvelous. What is revelation? The testimony of the Father and Son. How many of you have had revelation? How many of you have had the Spirit of God whisper unto you—the still small voice. I would have been in the spirit world a great many years ago, if I had not followed the promptings of the still small voice. These were the revelations of Jesus Christ, the strongest testimony a man or a woman can have. I have had many testimonies since I have been connected with this Church and kingdom. I have been blessed at times with certain gifts and graces, certain revelations and ministrations; but with

them all I have never found anything that I could place more dependence upon than the still small voice of the Holy Ghost.
— *3 July 1880, Journal of Discourses, 21:195–96.*

TEMPLES FOR THE SAVIOR'S WORK. This is a preparation necessary for the second advent of the Savior; and when we shall have built the temples now contemplated, we will then begin to see the necessity of building others, for in proportion to the diligence of our labors in this direction, will we comprehend the extent of the work to be done, and the present is only a beginning. When the Savior comes, a thousand years will be devoted to this work of redemption; and temples will appear all over this land of Joseph — North and South America — and also in Europe and elsewhere; and all the descendants of Shem, Ham, and Japheth, who received not the gospel in the flesh, must be officiated for in the Temples of God, before the Savior can present the kingdom to the Father, saying, "It is finished."
— *16 September 1877, Journal of Discourses, 19:229–230.*

DREAMS AND VISIONS. I was in Tennessee in the year 1835, and while at the house of Abraham O. Smoot, I received a letter from Brothers Joseph Smith and Oliver Cowdery, requesting me to stay there, and stating that I would lose no blessing by doing so. Of course, I was satisfied. I went into a little room and sat down upon a small sofa. I was all by myself and the room was dark; and while I rejoiced in this letter and the promise made to me, I became wrapped in vision. I was like Paul; I did not know whether I was in the body or out of the body. A personage appeared to me and showed me the great scenes that should take place in the last days. One scene after another passed before me. I saw the sun darkened; I saw the moon become as blood; I saw the stars fall from heaven; I saw seven golden lamps set in the heavens, representing the various dispensations of God to man — a sign that would appear before the coming of Christ. I saw the resurrection of the dead. In the first resurrection those that came forth from their graves seemed to be all dressed alike, but in the second resurrection they were as diverse in their dress as this congregation is before me to-day, and if I had been an artist I could have painted the whole scene as it was impressed upon my mind, more indelibly fixed than anything I had ever seen with the natural eye. What does this mean? It was a testimony of the resurrection of the dead. I had a testimony. I believe in the resurrection of the dead, and I know it is a true principle. . . . But what I wanted to say in regard to these matters is, that the Lord does communicate some things of importance to the children of men by means of visions and dreams as well as by the records of divine truth. And what is it all for? It is to teach us a principle. We may never see anything take place exactly as we see it in a dream or a vision, yet it is intended to teach us a principle. My dream gave me a strong testimony of the resurrection. I am satisfied, always have been, in regard to the resurrection. I rejoice in it. The way was opened unto us by the blood of the Son of God.

    —8 October 1881, Journal of Discourses, 22:332–33.

FIVE WISE AND FIVE FOOLISH SAINTS. The parable of the ten virgins is intended to represent the second coming of the Son of Man, the coming of the Bridegroom to meet the bride, the Church, the Lamb's wife, in the last days; and I expect that the Savior was about right when he said, in reference to the members of the Church, that five of them were wise and five were foolish; for when the Lord of heaven comes in power and great glory to reward every man according to the deeds done in the body, if he finds one-half of those professing to be members of his Church prepared for salvation, it will be as many as can be expected, judging by the course that many are pursuing.

—*12 September 1875*, Journal of Discourses, *18:110.*

THEY VISIT YOU. If this is the work of the Lord, and if the God of Israel has set up a kingdom, undertaken to establish a Church and a Zion, I wish to ask—can the inhabitants of the earth help it? Can they hinder it? Can they stay the hand of the Lord? I wish the world to reflect upon these things. Or will the unbelief of the world make the truth of God without effect? Judge ye. Joseph Smith, while in Liberty Jail, while in chains and imprisoned, prayed to the Lord . . . and the Lord answered his prayer. He told him a great many things, among the rest that all things should be revealed in the days of the dispensation of the fulness of times, according to that which was ordained in the midst of the Council of the Eternal God of all other Gods, before the world was—all these things should be revealed in the latter days. Now, says the Lord, "How long can rolling waters remain impure? What power shall stay the heavens? As well might man stretch forth his puny arm to stop the Missouri River in its decreed course, or to turn it up stream, as to hinder the Almighty from pouring down knowledge from heaven upon the heads of the Latter-day Saints." . . .

The eyes of the heavenly hosts are over us; the eyes of God himself and his son Jesus Christ and all those apostles and prophets who have sealed their testimony with their blood are watching this people. They visit you, they observe your works, for they know very well that your destiny is to build up this Kingdom, to build up Zion, sanctify it, sanctify the earth and prepare the world for the coming of the Son of Man. The judgments of God are at the door of the wicked; they cannot hinder them. . . . The Lord is watching over you, and he will sustain his work.

I know that Joseph Smith was a prophet of God, and he sealed his testimony with his blood. That testimony is in force upon all the world, and it will cost this generation just as much to shed the blood of the Lord's anointed to-day as it has cost the Jews for shedding the blood of Jesus Christ eighteen hundred years ago. The Jews have been scattered, they have been under the bondage of the Gentiles for all these years, and they have until recently been denied all political rights. But the Lord is about to restore them. This is the Kingdom of God. It is the Gospel of Jesus Christ.

— *In Conference Report of The Church of Jesus Christ of Latter-day Saints, April 1880, pp. 82, 85.*

THE COMING OF THE SON OF MAN TO THIS GENERATION. The signs of heaven and earth all indicate the near coming of the son of Man. You read the 9th, 10th, and 11th chapters of the last Book of Nephi, and see what the Lord has said will take place in this generation, when the gospel of Christ has again been offered to the inhabitants of the earth. The Lord did not reveal the day of the coming of the son of Man, but he revealed the generation. That generation is upon us. The signs of heaven and earth predict the fulfillment of these things, and they will come to pass.

— *3 July 1880, Journal of Discourses, 21:195.*

JESUS CHRIST WAS INVINCIBLE. When Jesus Christ came to the Jews he brought the everlasting Gospel. He was of the tribe of Judah himself. He came to his own father's house; he offered them life and salvation; yet he was the most unpopular man in all Judah. The High Priests, the Saducees, the sectarians of the day, were the strongest enemies he had on earth. No matter what he did, it was imputed to an evil source. When he cast out devils it was imputed to the power of Belzebub, the prince of devils. When he opened the eyes of the blind they said: "Give God the praise: we know that this man is a sinner." This unpopularity followed the Lord Jesus Christ to the cross where he gave up the ghost. Now, the inhabitants of Judah had an idea that if they could only put to death the Messiah, that that would end his mission and work on the earth. Vain hope of that generation as well as this! When they led Jesus to the cross, the very moment that spirit departed from that sorrowful tabernacle, it held the keys of the kingdom of God in all of its strength and power and glory the same as he had done while in the body. And while the body lay in the tomb, Jesus of Nazareth went and preached to the spirits in prison, and when his mission was ended there, his spirit returned again to his tabernacle. Did the Jews kill the principles he taught? No. He burst the bonds of death, he conquered the tomb, and came forth with an immortal body filled with glory and eternal life, holding all the powers and keys he held while in the flesh. Having appeared to some of the holy women and the apostles, he then went and administered to the Nephites upon this continent, and from here he went to the ten tribes of Israel, and delivered to them the Gospel, and when they return they will bring the history of the dealings of Jesus of Nazareth with them, while in his immortal body. The same unpopularity followed the twelve Apostles. Some of them were sawn asunder, others were beheaded, crucified, etc. But did the Jews destroy the principles they taught? Did they destroy the keys of the kingdom of God? No, verily no. They had no power over these things any more than they had power over the throne of God, or God Himself.

—*23 October 1881, Journal of Discourses, 22:343.*

CHRIST JESUS IS THE PATTERN. Those that live godly in Christ Jesus must suffer persecution. I believe myself, from the reading of the revelations of God, that it is necessary for

a people who are destined to inherit the celestial kingdom to
be a tried people. I have never read of the people of God in
any dispensation passing through life, as the sectarian world
would say, on flowery beds of ease, without opposition of any
kind. I have always looked upon the life of our Savior — who
descended beneath all things that He might rise above all
things — as an example for His followers. And yet it has always,
in one sense of the word, seemed strange to me that the Son
of God, the First Begotten in the eternal worlds of the Father,
and the Only Begotten in the flesh, should have to descend to
the earth and pass through what He did — born in a stable,
cradled in a manger, persecuted, afflicted, scorned, a hiss and
bye-word to almost all the world, and especially to the inhabitants of Jerusalem and Judea. There was apparently nothing that the Savior could do that was acceptable in the eyes
of the world; anything and almost everything he did was
imputed to an unholy influence. . . . And so all his life
through, to the day of his death upon the cross. There is
something about all this that appears sorrowful; but it seemed
necessary for the Savior to descend below all things that he
might ascend above all things. So it has been with other men.
When I look at the history of Joseph Smith, I sometimes think
that he came as near following the footsteps of the Savior —
(although no more so than his disciples) — as any one possibly
could. Joseph Smith was called to lay down his life; he sealed
his testimony with his blood, and passed through some serious
trials and afflictions. In section 122 of the Book of Doctrine
and Covenants — the word of the Lord given to the Prophet
while in Liberty jail — the Lord showed him his condition and
position. He refers there to the trials and troubles he was
called to pass through, and then compares them with what
He Himself (the Savior) had to endure. He says: "And if thou
shouldst be cast into the pit, or into the hands of murderers,
and the sentence of death passed upon thee; if thou be cast

into the deep; if the billowing surge conspire against thee; if
fierce winds become thine enemy; if the heavens gather blackness, and all the elements combine to hedge up the way; and
above all, if the very jaws of hell shall gape, open the mouth
wide after thee, know thou, my Son, that all these things
shall give thee experience, and shall be for thy good. The
Son of man hath descended below them all; art thou greater
than He? Therefore, hold on thy way, and the Priesthood
shall remain with thee, for their bounds are set, they cannot
pass. Thy days are known, and thy years shall not be numbered
less; therefore, fear not what man can do, for God shall be
with you for ever and ever." The Lord showed him in this
revelation that these afflictions were necessary. We have been
called to pass through trials many times, and I do not think
we should complain, because if we had no trials we should
hardly feel at home in the other world in the company of the
Prophets and Apostles who were sawn asunder, crucified, etc.,
for the word of God and testimony of Jesus Christ. . . .

Do we comprehend that if we abide the laws of the Priesthood we shall become heirs of God and joint-heirs with Jesus
Christ? . . . Jesus Christ abode in the covenant; he kept all
the commandments while he was upon the earth. He even
was baptized by the hands of John, although it was not for
the remission of sin, but to fulfill all righteousness. There was
no part of the Gospel that Christ did not fulfill, and he called
upon Joseph Smith to fulfill the same. This he did. He laid
down his life. He went to the spirit world, and he is there
watching over this people. He has power there, and so have
our brethren who have gone to the other side of the veil.
They are laboring for us. They are watching to see how we
perform the work left to our charge.

— 10 December 1882, Journal of Discourses, *23:327– 28, 330.*

SIN ATONED FOR THROUGH CHRIST. The Savior came

and tabernacled in the flesh, and entered upon the duties of
the priesthood at 30 years of age. After laboring three and a
half years He was crucified and put to death in fulfillment of
certain predictions concerning him. He laid down his life as
a sacrifice for sin, to redeem the world. When men are called
upon to repent of their sins, the call has reference to their
own individual sins, not to Adam's transgressions. What is
called the original sin was atoned for through the death of
Christ irrespective of any action on the part of man; also man's
individual sin was atoned for by the same sacrifice, but on
condition of his obedience to the Gospel plan of salvation
when proclaimed in his hearing.
    —Millennial Star, 51 (1889): 659.

BE ONE. "If ye are not one ye are not mine." The subject
that I have upon my mind is, union among the Latter-day
Saints. The Savior said to his apostles anciently, and to the
apostles in our day: "I say unto you, be one; and if ye are not
one ye are not mine." "I and my Father are one." With all
the divisions, and all the discontent, and the quarrelings and
opposition among the powers on earth, or that have been
revealed from heaven, I have never heard that it has ever
been revealed to the children of men that there was any
division between God the Father, God the Son, and God the
Holy Ghost. They are one. They always have been one. They
always will be one, from eternity unto eternity. Our Heavenly
Father stands at the head, being the Author of the salvation
of the children of men, having created and peopled the world
and given laws to the inhabitants of the earth. This principle
is shown unto us by the revelation of the laws which belong
to the different kingdoms. There is a celestial kingdom, a
terrestrial kingdom, and a telestial kingdom. There is a glory
of the sun, a glory of the moon, and a glory of the stars; and
as one star differs from another star in glory, so also is the

resurrection of the dead. In the celestial kingdom of God there is oneness — there is union.

 — Millennial Star, *52 (1890): 577.*

HOW TO OBTAIN REVELATIONS FROM THE LORD. In order to obtain revelation from God, and in order to know when we do obtain revelation, whether it is from God or not, we must follow the teachings of the revelations of God unto us. . . .

Joseph Smith went before the Lord and prayed in the name of Jesus Christ, and asked for knowledge, wisdom and understanding in order to know what to do to be saved; and he proved the promises of St. James [see James 1:5] before the Lord, and the heavens were opened to his view, and the Father and the Son were revealed unto him, and the voice of the great Eloheim unto him was: "This is my beloved Son, hear ye Him."

This was the first revelation of God to him. He did hearken to the voice of Jesus Christ all his life afterwards, and received a code of revelations and the word of the Lord unto him as long as he dwelt in the flesh.

Joseph Smith left as strong a testimony as was ever given to the human family, and sealed that testament with his own life and blood.

We all have to pursue the very same course in order to obtain revelations from God. But I wish to impress this truth upon the rising generation and all who read this testimony, that the Lord does not give revelations or send angels to men or work miracles to accommodate the notions of any man who is seeking for a sign.

When we have the principles of the gospel revealed to us through the mouth of the Savior, or by inspired prophets or apostles, we have no need to ask the Lord to reveal that unto us again. . . .

When any priest, elder, prophet, apostle, or messenger is sent of God to preach the gospel, gather the Saints, work in temples or perform any work for the Lord, and that man is faithful and humble before the Lord in his prayers and duty, and there is any snare or evil in his path, or the righteous to be sought out, or danger to the emigration of the Saints either by sea or land, or knowledge needed in a temple, then the Lord will reveal to him all that is necessary to meet the emergency.

—Leaves from My Journal, 93–95.

THE LORD WILL NOT LEAD YOU ASTRAY. The Lord will never permit me or any other man who stands as President of this Church to lead you astray. It is not in the programme. It is not in the mind of God. If I were to attempt that, the Lord would remove me out of my place, and so He will any other man who attempts to lead the children of men astray from the oracles of God and from their duty.

—Deseret Evening News, *11 October 1890, p. 2.*

THE SON OF GOD DECREED THAT IT MUST BE SO. I feel disposed to say something with regard to the Manifesto. To begin with, I will say this work was like a mountain upon me. I saw by the inspiration of Almighty God what lay before this people, and I knew that something had to be done to ward off the blow that I saw impending. But I should have let come to pass what God showed me by revelation and vision; I should have lived in the flesh and permitted these things to come to pass; I should have let this temple go into the hands of our enemies; I should have let every temple be confiscated by the hands of the wicked; I should have permitted all Church property to have been confiscated by our enemies; I should have seen these people — prophets and apostles — driven by our enemies, and our wives and children scattered to the four winds of heaven. I should have seen all this had not Almighty God commanded me to do what I did. . . .

Now I will tell you what was manifested to me and what the Son of God performed in this thing. The Lord has never yet taken from Lucifer, the Son of the Morning, his agency. He still holds it and will hold it until he is bound with the keys of death and hell. The Devil still has power; and the Son of God knew full well if something was not done in order to check this, all these things I have referred to would have come to pass. Yes, I saw by vision and revelation this Temple in the hands of the wicked. I saw our city in the hands of the wicked. I saw every temple in these valleys in the hands of the wicked. I saw great destruction among the people. All these things would have come to pass, as God Almighty lives, had not that Manifesto been given. Therefore, the Son of God felt disposed to have that thing presented to the Church and to the world for purposes in his own mind. The Lord had decreed the establishment of Zion. He had decreed the finishing of his temple. He had decreed that the salvation of the living and the dead should be given in these valleys of the mountains. And Almighty God decreed that the Devil should not thwart it."

—April 1893 sermon by Wilford Woodruff, fourth session of dedicatory services of the Salt Lake Temple, in The Discourses of Wilford Woodruff, ed. G. Homer Durham (Salt Lake City: Bookcraft, 1946), 217–18.

CHRIST IS CHRIST. In speaking of the Apostles and Prophets that were with Joseph Smith when he made his last speech, I am the only man living that was with him at that time. The rest are to-day in the spirit world. How much longer I shall talk to his people I do not know; but I want to say this to all Israel: Cease troubling yourselves about who God is; who Adam is, who Christ is, who Jehovah is. For heaven's sake, let these things alone. Why trouble yourselves about these things? God has revealed Himself, and when the 121st section of the Doctrine and Covenants is fulfilled, whether there be one God or many gods they will be revealed to the children of men, as well as all thrones and dominions, principalities, and powers. Then why trouble yourselves about these things? God is God. Christ is Christ. The Holy Ghost is the Holy Ghost. That should be enough for you and me to know. If we want to know any more, wait till we get where God is in person. . . . Humble yourselves before the Lord; seek for light, for truth, and for a knowledge of the common things of the kingdom of God. The Lord is the same yesterday, to-day, and forever. He changes not. The Son of God is the same. He is the Savior of the world. He is our advocate with the Father.

—Millennial Star, *57 (1895): 355–56.*

HAND OF THE LORD. We ought to be thankful to the Lord for His mercies unto us. I feel as though His hand has been visible in the establishing of His Church here in the Rocky Mountains, from our first arrival as Pioneers in the valleys of the mountains, when we found a barren desert, until the present. The hand of the Lord has been with this people and with the Elders of Israel, and will continue to be. The Lord is in earnest, in fulfillment of His promises from the creation of the world down to this day with regard to His dispensations to man. I hope and trust that while we dwell in the flesh we all may realize and understand this. It is a great blessing to receive the Gospel of Christ, to receive the Holy Priesthood, and to be called to labor in the Priesthood for the salvation of the children of men. This labor is upon us and will remain upon us until the coming of the Son of Man in the clouds of heaven, to reward every man according to the deeds done in the body.

—In Conference Report, *October 1897, pp. 1–2.*

Chapter 5

LORENZO SNOW

Born: 3 April 1814
Ordained an Apostle: 12 February 1849
Ordained President: 13 September 1898
Died: 10 October 1901

WE ARE DEPENDENT UPON JESUS CHRIST. Now it is
so ordered and so arranged, that we are dependent, in a great
measure, one upon another. For instance, take us as a people,
we are dependent upon a being that is above us to secure our
peace, our happiness, our glory, and exaltation; we are in-
dividually dependent upon the exertions of an individual who
is above ourselves.

For instance, we are all dependent upon Jesus Christ, upon
his coming into the world to open the way whereby we might
secure peace, happiness, and exaltation. And had he not made
these exertions, we never could have been secured in these
blessings and privileges which are guaranteed unto us in the

Gospel, through the mediation of Jesus Christ, for he made the necessary exertions.

In order to accomplish the gathering of Israel out of Egyptian bondage, there had to be something done to liberate them from their thraldom, and this something had to be done by a higher power, by an individual that had more wisdom, more intelligence, more understanding, and more power and means within his hands for the purpose of securing those blessings which they needed. They never could have got out from their difficulties nor from their bondage, unless this power had been exerted by one who had more intelligence, more knowledge, more information in relation to the means of their deliverance.

It is just so in a thousand other cases, there has to be a power exercised for the benefit of the people, there has to be exertions made, and they never can receive the blessings and privileges that are for them, unless those exertions were made by an individual possessing more knowledge, more wisdom, and greater power than themselves.

Jesus, on a certain occasion, speaking to Peter, said to him, "Simon Peter, lovest thou me?" he answered that he did. Well, then, replied Jesus, "feed my sheep." Jesus interrogated him again, saying, "Simon Peter, lovest thou me?" Peter answered, "I do, Lord." Jesus said unto him, "Feed my lambs." In this case we perceive there was an exertion to be made for the benefit of those that had not that power and information, but this alone is not sufficient.

Had Moses, for instance, having done all that he did, had he delivered Israel from Egyptian bondage, and having done all that he could and all that mortal man could do for their redemption, having done all in his power, and been willing to lay down his life and to sacrifice everything that he had to accomplish that work, would he have secured the people to himself, and have brought about that union which was so necessary, without any exertion on their part? No, most assuredly it would not have been accomplished, for there had to be a return, an exertion on their part, in order to secure that union and that love, and to secure that fellowship between them and him, which it was necessary should exist, and so it is in reference to Jesus Christ, though he has sacrificed himself and laid the plan for the redemption of the people, yet unless the people labour to obtain that union between him and them, their salvation never will be accomplished. Thus we see that some thing has to be done by each party, in order to secure each other's friendship, and to bind us together as a community.

—*1 March 1857,* Journal of Discourses, 4:239–40.

JESUS SOUGHT TO HONOR THE FATHER. Jesus, while travelling here on earth, fulfilling his mission, told the people he did not perform the miracles he wrought in their midst by his own power, nor by his own wisdom; but he was there in order to accomplish the will of his Father. He came not to seek the glory of men, and the honor of men; but to seek the honor and glory of his Father that sent him. Said he, "I am come in my Father's name, and ye receive me not, if another shall come in his own name, him ye will receive."

Now, the peculiarity of his mission, and that which distinguished it from other missions, was this: he came not to seek the honor and glory of men, but to seek the honor and glory of his Father, and to accomplish the work of his Father who sent him. Herein lay the secret of his prosperity; and herein lies the secret of the prosperity of every individual who works upon the same principle.

—*9 October 1869,* Journal of Discourses, 13:254.

STATE OF PERFECTION. The Latter-day Saints expect to arrive at this state of perfection; we expect to become as our Father and God, fit and worthy children to dwell in his presence; we expect that when the Son of God shall appear, we shall receive our bodies renewed and glorified, and that "these vile bodies will be changed and become like unto his glorious body."

—*7 April 1879, Journal of Discourses, 20:189.*

HOW I GAINED A TESTIMONY. I have been over fifty years . . . actively engaged in bearing witness of my knowledge respecting the divine authenticity of what is called Mormonism, and have declared the principles of my religion and borne my testimony of them through various portions of my own country, also in Great Britain, Scotland, Wales, Ireland, France, Italy, Switzerland, Austria, Germany, Turkey, Land of Palestine, and on the islands of the sea. These arduous and sacred responsibilities would never have been ventured by me without first *knowing* this religion, this gospel, and the authority to preach it had come direct from God to Joseph Smith, pure and unadulterated; not simply a *belief* but a *knowledge* direct to me from God himself. . . .

In speaking of knowledge I employ the term in its literal sense. I mean a physical demonstration, not belief alone, a feeling arising merely from mental enlightenment, as you mention, but a physical knowledge, through the organ of the senses, of a nature which could never be questioned or doubted by its possessor while life and memory exist. . . .

Being at that time a young man, full of worldly aspirations, with bright prospects, and means to gratify my ambition in acquiring a liberal collegiate education; also having a host of wealthy, proud, aristocratic friends and relatives watching eagerly for my achieving high honors in life, of course you can easily understand that it was a great trial, and required the strongest effort to form a resolution to abandon those prospects, disappoint expectations, join the poor, ignorant despised Mormons, and follow Old Joe Smith, the money digger, as he and they were regarded.

Had I then understood, as I now *know,* the ultimate results of obedience to the gospel, a life of purity, and after its close an exaltation to the fullness of the Godhead, I should then have been ashamed to have called it a sacrifice. But in my ignorance, at that time, of its blessings and glories, it proved the fiercest struggle of heart and will I ever experienced before or since. But through the help of the Lord, for I feel certain that He must have helped me, I laid my pride, worldly ambition and aspirations upon the altar, and as humble as a child went to the waters of baptism, received the ordinance administered by an Apostle, and afterwards the laying on of hands.

One evening, a few days after this, when alone, engaged in earnest prayer, the heavens were opened, the veil was rent from my mind, and then and there I received the most wonderful manifestations, grand and sublime, I believe as man was ever permitted to receive, and beyond the power of language fully to describe. It was shown me in that vision that there truly existed a Son of God, that Joseph Smith was really a prophet of God.

The first intimation of the approach of that marvelous vision was a sound just above my head like the rustling of silken robes, when immediately the Holy Spirit descended upon me, enveloping my whole person, filling me from the crown of my head to the so[le]s of my feet, which was a complete baptism, as tangible an immersion in a heavenly principle or element — the Holy Ghost — infinitely more real, physical in its effects upon every part of my system than was the immersion when I was baptized in water. That night after retiring to rest the same wonderful manifestations were repeated, and continued to be for several successive nights. From that time till the present on numerous occasions miraculous manifestations of the divine power have followed me and my administrations of the gospel ordinances. . . . I profess to have, and *actually* do have, the right and authority from God to administer this gospel, and promise the Holy Ghost and divine knowledge to follow all who accept it with sincerity and purity of heart.

    —*"How I Gained My Testimony of the Truth,"* The Young Woman's Journal, 4 (9 October 1886): 215–17.

FOR THE SALVATION OF THE WORLD. In the days of Noah very few indeed received the truth which God revealed. In the days of the Son of God very few would receive His testimony. In these days very few receive the testimony that God has revealed His Gospel and has required His servants to declare it to the world. It is strange indeed—and yet perhaps not so strange, when we consider the circumstances. When Jesus lay in the manger, a helpless infant, He knew not that He was the Son of God, and that formerly He created the earth. When the edict of Herod was issued, He knew nothing of it; He had not power to save Himself; and His father and mother had to take Him and fly into Egypt to preserve Him from the effects of that edict. Well, He grew up to manhood, and during His progress it was revealed unto Him who He was, and for what purpose He was in the world. The glory and power He possessed before He came into the world was made known unto Him. It was not a very pleasurable thing to be placed upon the cross and to suffer the excruciating torture that He bore for hours, in order to accomplish the work for which He had come upon the earth. It has not been with the Latter-day Saints the most delightful thing that could be imagined to suffer as they have suffered—and what for? For the same as Jesus suffered, to a certain extent—for the salvation of the world.

    —*In Conference Report, 6 April 1901, p. 3.*

HIS FATHER HAD EDUCATED HIM. As we move forward
in eternity and along the line of our existence, we shall be
placed in certain conditions that require very great sacrifice
in the interests of humanity, in the interests of the Spirit of
God, in the interest of His children and our own children,
in generations to come, in eternity. Jesus Christ the Son of
God was once placed in a condition that it required the highest
effort in order to accomplish what was necessary for the salvation of millions of the children of God. It required the
highest effort and determination that had to be exercised
before the Son of God could pass through the ordeal, the
sacrifice that was necessary.

I believe that his Father had educated him, had passed
him through scenes that were of a very serious character, of
great trials, and he knew just what he could depend upon from
the facts that were illustrated and shown by his experience. . . .

That is just the way the Lord intends to do with you or
me exactly. We will be judged according to what we have
done or what we have failed to have done all along the line
of our experiences. When Jesus was placed in a condition
where acting in propriety or otherwise confronted him; when
he saw before Him the cross and the immediate prospects of
being placed upon it and of his undergoing those excruciating
tortures that he had seen others experiencing, then his nature
failed as it were and he said: Father if it be possible that this
experience or this cup pass from me, let it pass.

That is the way he told the Lord. But notwithstanding,
he said: If this cannot be done, Thy will be done, and not
mine. So he was placed upon the cross and suffered that
excruciating torture. Supposing that he had failed, the nations
of the earth and the people of the Lord, his sons and daughters,
would have failed to be put into the position of having the
opportunity that you and I have today. They would have failed

for a long time, to say the least. Of course the provisions would have been made and the work of the Almighty would have been proceeded with, but there would have been a halt there. But the Lord knew just what he could depend upon, and therefore, he selected that son of His, our Savior, Jesus Christ, and he has wrought out that great work of redemption for the human family, the living and the dead.

—In Conference Report, 5 October 1900, pp. 2–3.

DIVINE MANIFESTATIONS TO LORENZO SNOW, RE-
LATED BY HIS SON LE ROI C. SNOW. In 1836, when Lorenzo Snow was twenty-two years of age, and two weeks before he joined the Church, he says: "It was at my sister's (Eliza R. Snow's) invitation that I attended a patriarchal bless-ing meeting conducted by Father Smith, in the Kirtland temple. I listened with astonishment to him telling the breth-ren and sisters their parentage, their lineage, and other things which I could not help but believe he knew nothing about, save as the Spirit manifested them unto him." . . .

Six months later Lorenzo Snow, himself, received a pa-triarchal blessing from Father Smith. Among many other mi-raculous statements and promises were these: "Thou hast a great work to perform. Thou shalt become a mighty man. There shall not be a mightier man on the earth than thou. Thou shalt have long life; the vigor of thy mind shall not be abated and the vigor of thy body shall be preserved. Thou shalt have power to stand in the flesh and see Jesus."

For some time President Woodruff's health had been fail-ing. Nearly every evening President Lorenzo Snow visited him at his home on South 5th East Street. This particular evening the doctors said President Woodruff was failing rapidly and they feared he would not live much longer.

Lorenzo Snow was then President of the Council of the Twelve and was greatly worried over the possibility of suc-

ceeding President Woodruff, especially because of the terrible
financial condition of the Church. Referring to this condition
President Heber J. Grant has said: "The Church was in a
financial slough of despond, so to speak, almost financially
bankrupt—its credit was hardly good for a thousand dollars
without security."

My father went to his room in the Salt Lake Temple where
he was residing at the time. He dressed in his robes of the
Priesthood, went into the Holy of Holies, there in the House
of the Lord and knelt at the sacred altar. He plead with the
Lord to spare President Woodruff's life, that President Woodruff might outlive him and that the great responsibility of
Church leadership would never fall upon his shoulders. Yet
he promised the Lord that he would devotedly perform any
duty required at his hands. At this time he was in his eighty-
sixth year.

Soon after this President Woodruff was taken to California
where he died Friday morning at 6:40 o'clock September 2nd,
1898. President George Q. Cannon at once wired the sad
information to the President's office in Salt Lake City. Word
was forwarded to President Snow who was in Brigham City.
The telegram was delivered to him on the street in Brigham.
He read it to President Rudger Clawson, then president of
Box Elder Stake, who was with him, went to the telegraph
office and replied that he would leave on the train about 5:30
that evening. He reached Salt Lake City about 7:15, proceeded
to the President's office, gave some instructions and then went
to his private room in the Salt Lake Temple.

President Snow put on his holy temple robes, repaired
again to the same sacred altar, offered up the signs of the
Priesthood and poured out his heart to the Lord. He reminded
the Lord how he had plead for President Woodruff's life and
that his days might be lengthened beyond his own; that he
might never be called upon to bear the heavy burdens and

responsibilities of Church leadership. "Nevertheless," he said,
"Thy will be done. I have not sought this responsibility but
if it be Thy will, I now present myself before Thee for Thy
guidance and instruction. I ask that Thou show me what thou
wouldst have me do."

After finishing his prayer, he expected a reply, some special
manifestation from the Lord. So he waited — and waited — and
waited. There was no reply, no voice, no visitation, no manifestation. He left the altar and the room in great disappoint-
ment. He passed through the Celestial room and out into the
large corridor leading to his own room where a most glorious
manifestation was given President Snow. One of the most
beautiful accounts of this experience is told by his granddaughter, Allie Young Pond.

"One evening when I was visiting Grandpa Snow in his
room in the Salt Lake Temple, I remained until the door-
keepers had gone and the night-watchman had not yet come
in, so grandpa said he would take me to the main, front
entrance and let me out that way. He got his bunch of keys
from his dresser.

"After we left his room and while we were still in the large
corridor, leading into the celestial room, I was walking several
steps ahead of grandpa when he stopped me saying: 'Wait a
moment Allie, I want to tell you something. It was right here
that the Lord Jesus Christ appeared to me at the time of the
death of President Woodruff. He instructed me to go right
ahead and reorganize the First Presidency of the Church at
once and not wait as had been done after the death of the
previous presidents, and that I was to succeed President Woodruff.'

"Then grandpa came a step nearer and held out his left
hand and said 'He stood right here, about three feet above
the floor. It looked as though He stood on a plate of solid
gold.'

"Grandpa told me what a glorious personage the Savior is and described His hands, feet, countenance and beautiful, white robes, all of which were of such a glory of whiteness and brightness that he could hardly gaze upon Him.

"Then grandpa came another step nearer me and put his right hand on my head and said: 'Now, granddaughter, I want you to remember that this is the testimony of your grandfather, that he told you with his own lips that he actually saw the Savior here in the Temple, and talked with Him face to face.'

"Then we went on and grandpa let me out of the main, front door of the Temple."

During the M.I.A. June conference in 1919 at the officers' testimony meeting in the Assembly Hall I [Le Roi Snow] related Allie Young Pond's experience and testimony. President Heber J. Grant immediately arose and said:

"In confirmation of the testimony given by Brother LeRoi C. Snow quoting the granddaughter of Lorenzo Snow, I want to call attention to the fact that several years elapsed after the death of the Prophet Joseph Smith before President Young was sustained as the president of the Church; after the death of President Young, several years elapsed again before President Taylor was sustained, and again when he died several years elapsed before President Woodruff was sustained.

"After the funeral of President Wilford Woodruff the Apostles met in the office of the First Presidency and Brother Francis M. Lyman said: 'I feel impressed although one of the younger members of the quorum, to say that I believe it would be pleasing in the sight of the Lord if the First Presidency of the Church was reorganized right here and right now. If I am in error regarding this impression, President Snow and the senior members of the council can correct me.

"President Snow said that he would be pleased to hear from all the brethren upon this question, and each and all of us expressed ourselves as believing it would be pleasing to the

Lord and that it would be the proper thing to have the Presidency organized at once.

"When we had finished, then and not till then, did Brother Snow tell us that he was instructed of the Lord in the Temple the night after President Woodruff died, to organize the Presidency of the Church at once. President Anthon H. Lund and myself are the only men now living who were present at that meeting.

"May the Lord bless and guide us by his spirit continually and may the testimony that we possess of the divinity of the work ever abide with us and may our faithfulness be an inspiration to lead others to a knowledge of the Gospel, is my prayer and I ask it in the name of Jesus Christ. Amen."

A few days later after the M.I.A. conference, in an interview with President Lund in his office he told the incident to me as given by President Grant regarding the meeting in the office of the First Presidency, which was held Tuesday morning, September 13, 1898, at which time Lorenzo Snow was chosen President of the Church. President Lund also told me that he heard my father tell a number of times, of the Savior's appearance to him, after he had dressed in his Temple robes, presented himself before the Lord and offered up the signs of the Priesthood.

I related this experience in the Eighteenth Ward Sacramental service. After the meeting Elder Arthur Winter told me he also had heard my father tell of the Savior's appearance to him in the Temple instructing him not only to reorganize the First Presidency at once but also to select the same counselors who had served with President Woodruff, Presidents George Q. Cannon and Joseph F. Smith.

Tuesday, September 13, 1898, eleven days after President Woodruff's death and five days after his funeral the Council of the Apostles met at 10 o'clock a.m. in the President's Office.

The special object of this meeting was to discuss the matter of borrowing for the Church, $1,500,000 in the East, because of its terrible financial condition. It was evident to the Council that nothing could be done legally in negotiating this loan until a new Trustee-in-trust had been sustained.

During the discussion Elder Lyman said: "If the Lord should manifest to you, President Snow, that it is the proper thing to do now, I am prepared not only to vote for a Trustee-in-trust, but for the President of the Church also, giving the President time, if he desires it, in which to choose his counselors." He remarked that after the death of Joseph Smith, three years elapsed before the First Presidency was organized; after the death of President Young, it also took three years to organize the First Presidency; after the death of President Taylor, eighteen months elapsed.

Elder Heber J. Grant remarked that the present time was just as opportune as any other, and that he could sustain President Snow with all his heart as President of the Church. Elder Young remarked that Brother Grant had expressed his feelings exactly.

Elder Teasdale said that he was in perfect harmony and accord with the feelings of these brethren.

Joseph F. Smith then said: "I move that this be the sense of this meeting."

The motion being seconded, Present Snow asked if there were any further remarks, whereupon several of the brethren called for the question. Then President Snow asked Elder Joseph F. Smith to put the motion. This being done it was carried unanimously, and Lorenzo Snow was thus sustained by the Council of the Apostles, as President of the Church of Jesus Christ of Latter-day Saints.

President Snow then arose and said: There was no use in his making excuses as to inability, etc., in assuming the vast responsibilities involved in the position to which he had been elected. He felt that it was for him to do the very best he could and to depend upon the Lord. He knew the action taken by the Council was according to the mind and will of the Lord, who had shown and revealed to him, several days ago, that the First Presidency should be organized before the next conference. He had been feeling a little gloomy, and perhaps a little discouraged at the prospect, and the vast responsibility that would naturally fall upon him as president of the Twelve Apostles, and with this feeling he went before the Lord, offered up the signs of the Holy Priesthood and called upon Him to let light come to his mind. His prayer was answered, the Lord manifested unto him clearly what he should do; also in regard to the counselors he should select when he became president of the Church, "And," said he, "in accordance with the light given me, I now present to you the name of Geo. Q. Cannon as my first counselor, and that of Joseph F. Smith as my second counselor."

Several of the brethren, speaking at the same time, seconded the choice of counselors, and the brethren named expressed themselves upon the subject — Brother Cannon to the effect that he was willing to act in this capacity, or any other, if he could have the love and confidence of his brethren, and Brother Smith to the effect that since the Lord had manifested His will in this matter, he had nothing to say, except that he was perfectly willing to act in this or any other position, and would do all he could to sustain the hands of the president in righteousness before the Lord.

President Snow, before calling for the vote, said: "I have not mentioned this matter to any person, either man or woman. I wanted to see what the feelings of the brethren were. I wanted to see if the same spirit which the Lord manifested to me was in you. I had confidence in you that the Lord would indicate to you that this was proper and according to His mind and will.

"I do not feel that I should be over-anxious in regard to

anything pertaining to the work of the Lord. I had one revelation in my early career which became my guiding star, so
to speak, and which I have always had before my mind, expressed in the following couplet: 'As man now is, God once
was; As God now is, man may be.' That was revealed to me
with power; the Holy Ghost was upon me for a long time,
and I knew it was my privilege to become like Him whom I
afterwards knew was my Father and God. As John the Apostle
says, 'We are now the sons of God; when He shall appear we
shall be like Him,' etc. We must act, as far as we possibly
can, like God, while we are in the flesh, and I know we can
reach that degree of perfection.

"Now brethren, I shall do the best I can, as God shall
give me wisdom and power. I sense keenly my own weakness
and inability, but I appreciate the fact that God can make
strong. If I know my own heart, the administration about to
be ushered in shall not be known as Lorenzo Snow's, but as
God's, in and through Lorenzo Snow. It will become us as
servants of the Lord to go to work and meet the difficulties
before us, as the Lord shall aid and assist us. I feel to say in
my heart, God bless you, and I invoke the blessing of the
Lord upon myself in the discharge of the obligations resting
upon me."

The vote was then taken approving unanimously the president's choice of counselors.

Lorenzo Snow was then sustained as trustee-in-trust for
the Church. . . .

Sun, Sept. 18, 1898, five days after he was sustained by
the Council of the Apostles as president of the Church, Pres.
Snow said in the Salt Lake Tabernacle:

"I can assure you, brethren and sisters, that I had no
ambition to assume the responsibility which now rests upon
me. If I could have escaped it honorably I should never have

been found in my present position, but the Lord revealed to me that this was His will."
—*Le Roi C. Snow,* Deseret News/Church Department, *2 April 1938, pp. 3, 8.*

FOLLOWING A CALL FOR TITHING. We have had a glorious time, and the Lord has been with us. The Lord has been with us greatly and manifested His holy will. We have had a revelation from the Lord since we left Salt Lake City, as you all understand. This manifestation that the Lord has given to me, and that you have received and borne testimony to, can never be forgotten. I know it just as well as I know anything that I ever did know.

There are different ways in which persons may receive revelations. One way is to receive it powerfully by the Holy Ghost falling upon us. Then there is another way that comes to us just as clearly and just as fully as the way in which the Lord bestowed upon us this revelation, when the Spirit of the Lord rests upon us and fills us as from the crowns of our heads to the soles of our feet. Now, this which I have received was not with the power of God resting upon me from the crown of my head to the soles of my feet, as it was when He gave me a knowledge of this Gospel, or when He gave me a knowledge of this principle, "As man now is, God once was; as God now is, man may be." That came to me powerfully and suddenly, and I saw it just as clearly as I see this bench or see your faces. This revelation that was given to me, in regard to this matter of tithing that we have talked about in the different settlements, was given to me just as fully, and I know it just as clearly, as any manifestation the Lord ever gave me.

And this has got to go through all the Stakes of Zion; and you brethren and sisters will be called upon from time to time, perhaps, to bear testimony to this manifestation. This will be a matter of record that will go down to generations to come;

it will be eternal and everlasting. Every one of you that has been a member of this company will have this matter renewed to you, and you will see it clearly; and you will see one of the greatest revolutions that has ever been made since this Church was organized, in this matter. There are things connected with it that I can see in the future. God bless the members of this company, every one of you, that we may never forget what the Lord has manifested to us, and that which we shall see clearly.

—26 May 1899 address at Nephi to the members of the company who accompanied Lorenzo Snow on his trip to St. George and through the settlements from 15 to 27 May 1899, LDS Church Archives. Spelling and punctuation have been standardized.

Chapter 6

JOSEPH F. SMITH

Born: 13 November 1838
Ordained an Apostle: 1 July 1866
Sustained as President: 10 November 1901
Died: 19 November 1918

RECEIVE THE WITNESS. I want to say as a servant of God, independent of the testimonies of all men and of every book that has been written, that I have received the witness of the Spirit in my own heart, and I testify before God, angels and men, without fear of the consequences that I know that my Redeemer lives, and I shall see him face to face, and stand with Him in my resurrected body upon this earth, if I am faithful; for God has revealed this unto me. I have received the witness, and I bear my testimony, and my testimony is true.

—*2 February 1883*, Journal of Discourses, *24:81*.

THE POWER OF CHRIST AND HIS SPIRIT. It is by the

power of God that all things are made that have been made. It is by the power of Christ that all things are governed and kept in place that are governed and kept in place in the universe. It is the power which proceeds from the presence of the Son of God throughout all the works of his hands, that giveth light, energy, understanding, knowledge, and a degree of intelligence to all the children of men, strictly in accordance with the words in the Book of Job, "There is a spirit in man; and the inspiration of the Almighty giveth them understanding." . . .

Even Christ himself was not perfect at first; he received not a fulness at first, but he received grace for grace, and he continued to receive more and more until he received a fulness. Is not this to be so with the children of men? Is any man perfect? Has any man received a fulness at once? Have we reached a point wherein we may receive the fulness of God, of his glory and his intelligence? No; and yet if Jesus, the Son of God, and the Father of the heavens and the earth in which we dwell, received not a fulness at the first, but increased in faith, knowledge, understanding and grace until he received a fulness, is it not possible for all men that are born of women to receive little by little, line upon line, precept upon precept, until they shall receive a fulness, as he has received a fulness, and be exalted with him in the presence of the Father? . . .

The question is often asked, is there any difference between the Spirit of the Lord and the Holy Ghost? The terms are frequently used synonymously. We often say the Spirit of God when we mean the Holy Ghost; we likewise say the Holy Ghost when we mean the Spirit of God. The Holy Ghost is a personage in the Godhead, and is not that which lighteth every man that comes into the world. It is the Spirit of God which proceeds through Christ to the world, that enlightens every man that comes into the world, and that strives with the children of men, and will continue to strive with them, until it brings them to a knowledge of the truth and the possession of the greater light and testimony of the Holy Ghost. If, however, he receive that greater light, and then sin against it, the Spirit of God will cease to strive with him, and the Holy Ghost will wholly depart from him. . . .

The Lord bless you, and help us all to live our religion and to keep the commandments of God, that we may look upon his face, and that we may see the Redeemer when he shall come to the earth again; for he will come, and when he does come again he will not come as the meek and lowly Nazarene, without "where to lay his head," and without respect and honor, but he will come as God out of heaven, clothed with power, glory, justice, judgment and truth. He will come with the hosts of heaven, and he will receive those who have kept his commandments in the earth as the church prepared for the Bridegroom, while he will take vengeance upon the ungodly.

— 16 March 1902 Tabernacle address, Improvement Era, 11 (1907–8): 380–83, 387.

THE LORD SPEAKS TO MAN'S IMMORTAL SOUL. Whenever the Lord speaks to man, he speaks to his immortal soul, and satisfaction and unsurpassing peace and joy come to all who listen.

Happy is the man, indeed, who can receive this soul-satisfying testimony, and be at rest, and seek for no other road to peace than by the doctrines of Jesus Christ. . . . His perfected philosophy teaches also that it is better to suffer wrong than to do wrong, and to pray for our enemies and for those who despitefully use us. . . . No other philosopher has ever said as Jesus said, "Come unto me."

—Improvement Era, 7 (1903–4): 717.

WHO WOULD WELCOME CHRIST'S RULE? I believe in

God's law. I believe that it is his right to rule in the world. I believe that no man has or should have any valid objection in his mind to the government of God, and the rule of Jesus Christ, in the earth. Let us suppose, for a moment, that Christ were here and that he was bearing rule in the world. Who would come under his condemnation? Who would be subject to his chastening word? Who would be in disharmony or unfellowship with God? Would the righteous man? Would the virtuous man? the pure and virtuous woman? the pure and honest in heart? the upright? the straightforward? those who do the will of heaven? Would they be in rebellion to Christ's rule if He were to come here to rule? No. They would welcome the rule and reign of Jesus Christ in the earth. They would welcome His law and acknowledge His sovereignty, they would hasten to rally to His standard and to uphold the purpose and the perfection of His laws and of His righteousness. Who would, then, be recreant to the rule of Christ? The whore-monger, the adulterer, the liar, the sorcerer, he who bears false witness against his neighbor, he who seeks to take advantage of his brother and who would overcome and destroy him for his own worldly gain or profit; the murderer, the despiser of that which is good, the unbeliever in the eternities that lie before us; the atheist, perhaps, although I think that he would not be so far from Christ as some that profess to be teachers of His doctrines and advocates of His laws. . . . Such as these would be the people who would not welcome the reign of Jesus Christ. Are there any who profess to be Latter-day Saints in this class, and would fear to have Christ reign and rule?

—In Conference Report, April 1904, p. 4.

CHRIST WAS RICH. A wise provision of the early Christians [was] to set apart a time when they should celebrate the natal day of Christ. It has had the effect of turning men's thoughts

to him and to his doctrines and works. We are apt to forget
the character of the structure which he built; and some are
even prone to consider that his ideals are impracticable. Men
have said that the theories which he taught are beautiful, but
that under modern arrangements, these cannot be put into
practice.

In our day, there is a tendency to count men of little value
who are not rich in worldly means and influence; who can not
on this day bestow presents upon family and friends, and
extend such acts of charity as find their way to the newspapers.
But Christ, the ideal, the model, declared of himself: "The
foxes have holes, and the birds of the air have nests; but the
Son of man hath not where to lay his head." Yet now he is
of all value, and exercises all influence, for only through him
are we saved. But it was not the influence of wealth, nor the
lavish gifts of gold that made him rich and gave him power.
It was the spirit of his Father, the wealth of his inner soul.

Who that can not build a great house, or control vast
interests, in our day, is looked upon by those who can, as of
only small consequence and little use among men; but with
all his poverty, Christ was rich in help, for when the tempest
arose, and his disciples came to him in their anguish, calling,
"Lord, save us; we perish," he arose and rebuked the wind
and the sea, and there was a great calm, causing the men to
marvel at his power, that even the winds and the sea obey
him!

—Improvement Era, 8 (1904–5): 146.

DOING THE WILL OF CHRIST. I do not believe in the
ideas that we hear sometimes advanced in the world, that it
matters but little what men do in this time, if they will but
confess Christ at the end of their journey in life, that that is
all-sufficient, and that by so doing they will receive their
passport into heaven. I denounce this doctrine. It is unscrip-

tural, it is unreasonable, it is untrue, and it will not avail any man, no matter by whom this idea may be advocated; it will prove an utter failure unto men. As reasonable beings, as men and women of intelligence, we cannot help but admire and honor the doctrine of Jesus Christ, which is the doctrine of God, and which requires of every man and woman righteousness in their lives, purity in their thoughts, uprightness in their daily walk and conversation, devotion to the Lord, love of truth, love of their fellow-man, and above all things in the world the love of God. These were the precepts that were inculcated by the Son of God when He walked among His brethren in the meridian of time. He taught these precepts; He exemplified them in His life, and advocated continually the *doing* of the will of Him that sent Him. . . .

I testify to you that Joseph Smith was instrumental in the hand of the Lord in restoring God's truth to the world, and also the holy Priesthood, which is His authority delegated unto man. I know this is true, and I testify of it to you. To me it is all-in-all; it is my life, it is my light; it is my hope, and my joy; it gives me the only assurance that I have for exaltation, for my resurrection from death, with those whom I have loved and cherished in this life, and with those with whom my lot has been cast in this world. . . . I know that my Redeemer lives, and that He shall stand upon the earth in the latter day, and, as Job has expressed it, "Though worms shall destroy this body, yet in my flesh shall I see God."

—In *Conference Report*, October 1907, p. 3–5.

GOD'S REST. I want to bear my testimony . . . that as I believe in my own existence, I believe in the divinity of this latter-day work; as I know, and as I have reason to know, that I am here and that I live, so I believe and I have reason to know that God, my Father, lives, that Jesus lives and that Joseph Smith was raised up of God to lay the foundations of this work. My whole hope of life, my all is staked upon this proposition, and I accept it, with all my soul. . . .

I pray that we may all enter into God's rest — rest from doubt, from fear, from apprehension of danger, rest from the religious turmoil of the world; from the cry that is going forth, here and there — lo, here is Christ; lo, there is Christ; lo, He is in the desert, come ye out to meet Him. The man who has found God's rest will not be disturbed by these vagaries of men, for the Lord has told him, and does tell us: "Go not out to seek them. Go not out to hunt them, for when Christ shall come, He will come with the army of heaven with Him in the clouds of glory, and all eyes shall see Him." We do not need to be hunting for Christ here, or Christ there, or prophets here and prophets there. . . .

To the faithful Latter-day Saint is given the right to know the truth, as God knows it; and no power beneath the celestial kingdom can lead him astray, darken his understanding, becloud his mind or dim his faith or his knowledge of the principles of the gospel of Jesus Christ. It can't be done, for the light of God shines brighter than the illumination of falsehood and error, therefore, those who possess the light of Christ, the spirit of revelation and the knowledge of God, rise above all these vagaries in the world; they know of this doctrine, that it is of God and not of man.

—In Conference Report, October 1909, pp. 3, 8–9.

THE WITNESS OF THE SPIRIT OF GOD. I want to bear my testimony to you Latter-day Saints. I know that my Redeemer lives. We have all the testimony and all the evidence of this great and glorious truth, that the world has, that is, all that the so-called Christian world possesses; and, in addition to all that they have, we have the testimony of the inhabitants of this western continent, to whom the Savior appeared, and delivered His gospel, the same as He delivered it to the Jews. In addition to all this new testimony and the testimony of the holy scriptures from the Jews, we have the testimony of the modern Prophet, Joseph Smith, who saw the Father and the Son, and who has borne record of them to the world; whose testimony was sealed with his blood, and is in force upon the world today. We have the testimony of others who witnessed the presence of the Son of God, in the Kirtland temple, when He appeared to them there, and the testimony of Joseph and Sidney Rigdon, who declared that they were the last witnesses of Jesus Christ. Therefore, I say again, I know that my Redeemer lives; for in the mouths of these witnesses this truth has been established in my mind.

Beside these testimonies, I have received the witness of the Spirit of God in my own heart, which exceeds all other evidences, for it bears record to me, to my very soul, of the existence of my Redeemer, Jesus Christ. I know that He lives, and that in the last day He shall stand upon the earth, and that He shall come to the people who shall be prepared for Him, as a bride is prepared for the bridegroom, when He shall come. I believe in the divine mission of the Prophet Joseph Smith, and I have every evidence that I need — at least enough to convince me of the divinity of his mission.

— In Conference Report, October 1910, p. 4.

CHRIST REVEALED HIMSELF TO JOSEPH. What did Joseph reveal? He revealed, or has been the instrument in the hands of God of revealing to the world Jesus, the Son of God, in His own person. He has been the instrument in the hands of the Lord of bringing the light to the inhabitants of the world that God lives, that Christ lives, whom to know is life eternal, and whom the world have ignorantly worshiped as a myth, as something that fills the immensity of space, but is indescribable; a something that is almighty and all-powerful and all-present, but without personal existence. Joseph has revealed to the world that Jesus Christ who was crucified and rose again from the dead, is a personal Being, in whose likeness and image man is made, or is begotten in the world, and that the Father is a person in exact similitude to the Son. We have the history of the Son, given us by His disciples who sojourned with Him while He was in the mortal flesh; . . . that when He rose and identified Himself beyond the possibility of any doubt to the minds of those who witnessed and saw Him, and knew Him, and afterwards testified of Him to the world, that He was the same that was crucified, bearing the marks of the nails and of the spear in His body; that He was not a spirit; that He was flesh and bone as tangible as man, and that a spirit had not this flesh and bone as He had. He declared this to the world: This same physical, tangible entity called Jesus of Nazareth, the son of Mary and the Son of God, in His resurrected body, came to Joseph Smith, revealed Himself to Joseph Smith, the same God, the same Christ, the same Redeemer of the world that was crucified on Calvary; and, that God, the Father, is like His Son; that it would be inconsistent and impossible for a spirit to beget a man like Christ, and therefore the Father and the Son are the exact resemblance of each other.

—In Conference Report, October 1911, pp. 4–5.

WHAT CHRIST HAS DONE. I am converted to the Gospel of Christ; I believe in Jesus with all my soul. I cannot doubt the evidences of more than sixty years of my experience in the Church in preaching the Gospel. Everything has contributed to the confirmation of my faith in the divine mission of the prophet Joseph Smith, and in the glorious plan of life and salvation taught by the Son of God, both for the living and for the dead. . . .

Jesus Christ . . . came into the world with power to lay down His life and take it up again, the only Being sent from

God to earth who possessed the power to lay down His life and take it up again. To no other soul under heaven has this power been given, and He demonstrated the resurrection from death to life by His own example, and has freely offered the same deliverance to all the sons and daughters of God that ever lived on earth or that will ever live from henceforth.

Christ has opened up to the world, through faith and obedience, this hope of everlasting life and exaltation in His glorious kingdom. Who else has taught such doctrines as this? Who else has exemplified this power and has done the deed? . . .

Joseph the Prophet comes to us in this dispensation and declares that the heavens were opened to him and to his associates, and he saw and heard, and he declares as the last witness, who has seen and heard and knows, that Jesus is the Christ and the Redeemer of the world, even He who was born of Mary, crucified and rose again from the dead, and visited the inhabitants of this continent, as well as the inhabitants of the old continent as we call it, who also bear witness of Him.

—In *Conference Report*, October 1913, pp. 8–9.

THE SPIRIT OF HIS INFLUENCE IN OUR SOULS.

There is no community in the earth, go where you will, that lives so near to the doctrine of Jesus Christ as do the Latter-day Saints; and they do it because they have received Christ's gospel, and the spirit of Christ in their hearts, and the testimony of Jesus, which is the spirit of prophecy. . . .

We speak of the Savior, of Jesus, the Son of God. We feel safe and solid in Him, that our feet have rested on the very foundation of eternal truth, when the spirit of Christ is in our hearts.

I want to say to my brethren and sisters, that if there is a man in all the world that has received more deeply and more

94   JOSEPH F. SMITH

keenly in his soul the love of Christ than I have, I would love to see him. I would love to be associated with such a man. Christ is, indeed, the Savior of my soul, the Savior of mankind. He has sacrificed His life for us that we might be saved; He has broken the bands of death, and has bid defiance to the grave, and bids us follow Him. He has come forth from death unto life again. He has declared Himself to be the way of salvation, the light and the life of the world, and I believe it with all my heart. I not only believe it, but as I know that the sun shines, so I know that belief in Him inspires to good and not to evil; and as I know that His spirit prompts to purity of life, to honor, to uprightness, to honesty and to righteousness, and not to evil, so I know by all the proofs that it is possible for me to grasp that Jesus is the Christ, the Son of the living God, the Savior of mankind. . . .

What will this knowledge alone avail? It will avail this, that having received that testimony in my heart, having received in my soul the witness of the Spirit of the living God, that Jesus is the Christ, and I stop there and go no further, that very witness in my soul will add to my eternal damnation. Why? Because it is not only our duty to know that Jesus is the Christ but to keep the influence of His spirit in our souls. It is not only necessary to have His testimony in our hearts but it is necessary that we should *do* the things that He has commanded, and the works of righteousness that He did, in order that we may attain to the exaltation that is in store for His children who *do* as well as believe. . . .

We believe in the Lord Jesus, and in His divine saving mission in the world, and in the redemption, the marvelous, glorious redemption that He has wrought for the salvation of the children of men. We believe in Him and this constitutes the foundation of our faith. He is the foundation and chief corner stone of our religion. We are His by adoption, by being buried with Christ in baptism, by being born of the water and the spirit anew into the world, through the ordinances of the Gospel of Christ, and we are thereby God's children, heirs of God and joint heirs with Jesus Christ, through our adoption and faith. . . .

The love of your fellowmen, the spirit of forgiveness, and mercy for your fellow beings is required of you, as was exemplified in the prayer of the Savior upon the cross—"O, Father, forgive them, for they know not what they do." So let us think of our enemies, so let us pray for them. . . .

No *man* will lead God's people nor His work. God may choose men, and make them instruments in His hands for accomplishing His purposes, but the glory and honor and power will be due to the Father in whom rests the wisdom and the might to lead His people and take care of His Zion. I am not leading The Church of Jesus Christ of Latter-day Saints and I want this distinctly understood. No man did. Joseph did not do it; Brigham did not do it; neither did John Taylor, nor Wilford Woodruff, nor Lorenzo Snow; and Joseph F. Smith, least of them all, is not leading The Church of Jesus Christ of Latter-day Saints, and will not lead it. They were instruments in God's hands in accomplishing what they did. God did it through them. The honor and the glory is due to the Lord and not to them. We are only instruments whom God may choose and use to do His work. . . .

We do honor Joseph Smith. We do not worship him, we worship God, and we call upon His holy name as we have been directed in the gospel in the name of His Son. We call for mercy in the name of Jesus; we ask for blessings in the name of Jesus. We are baptized in the name of the Father, and of the Son and of the Holy Ghost. We are initiated into the church and kingdom of God in the name of the Father and the Son and of the Holy Ghost, and we worship the Father. . . .

Let us follow Christ as He followed the Father, and do

the things that He said for us to do, and all will be well with us.

—Young Women's Journal, *17 (1906): 340–45.*

A Sure Foundation. From my boyhood I have desired to learn the principles of the gospel in such a way and to such an extent that it would matter not to me who might fall from the truth, who might make a mistake, who might fail to continue to follow the example of the Master, my foundation would be sure and certain in the truths that I have learned though all men else go astray and fail of obedience to them. We all have heard of people who have pinned their faith to the arm of flesh, who have felt that their belief, their confidence and their love for the principles of the gospel of Jesus Christ would be shattered if their ideals—those possibly who first taught them the principles of the Gospel—should make a mistake, falter or fall.

I know of but one in all the world who can be taken as the first and only perfect standard for us to follow, and He is the Only Begotten Son of God. I would feel sorry, indeed, if I had friend or an associate in this life who would turn away from the plan of life and salvation because I might stumble or make a failure of my life. I want no man to lean upon me nor to follow me, only so far as I am a consistent follower in the footsteps of the Master.

—Juvenile Instructor, *50 (1915–16): 738–39.*

Vision of the Redemption of the Dead. The eyes of my understanding were opened, and the Spirit of the Lord rested upon me, and I saw the hosts of the dead, both small and great. And there were gathered together in one place an innumerable company of the spirits of the just, who had been faithful in the testimony of Jesus while they lived in mortality; and who had offered sacrifice in the similitude of the great sacrifice of the Son of God, and had suffered tribulation in their Redeemer's name. All these had departed the mortal life, firm in the hope of a glorious resurrection, through the grace of God the Father and his Only Begotten Son, Jesus Christ. . . .

While this vast multitude waited and conversed, rejoicing in the hour of their deliverance from the chains of death, the Son of God appeared, declaring liberty to the captives who had been faithful; and there he preached to them the everlasting gospel, the doctrine of the resurrection and the redemption of mankind from the fall, and from individual sins on conditions of repentance. But unto the wicked he did not go, and among the ungodly and the unrepentant who had defiled themselves while in the flesh, his voice was not raised; neither did the rebellious who rejected the testimonies and the warnings of the ancient prophets behold his presence, nor look upon his face.

Where these were, darkness reigned, but among the righteous there was peace; and the saints rejoiced in their redemption, and bowed the knee and acknowledged the Son of God as their Redeemer and Deliverer from death and the chains of hell. Their countenances shone, and the radiance from the presence of the Lord rested upon them, and they sang praises unto his holy name.

I marveled, for I understood that the Savior spent about three years in his ministry among the Jews and those of the house of Israel, endeavoring to teach them the everlasting gospel and call them unto repentance; and yet, notwithstanding his mighty works and miracles, and proclamation of the truth, in great power and authority, there were but few who hearkened to his voice, and rejoiced in his presence, and received salvation at his hands. But his ministry among those who were dead was limited to the brief time intervening between the crucifixion and his resurrection; and I wondered at the words of Peter—wherein he said that the Son of God preached unto the spirits in prison, who sometime were disobedient, when once the longsuffering of God waited in the days of Noah—and how it was possible for him to preach to those spirits and perform the necessary labor among them in so short a time.

And as I wondered, my eyes were opened, and my understanding quickened, and I perceived that the Lord went not in person among the wicked and the disobedient who had rejected the truth, to teach them; but behold, from among the righteous, he organized his forces and appointed messengers, clothed with power and authority, and commissioned them to go forth and carry the light of the gospel to them that were in darkness, even to all the spirits of men; and thus was the gospel preached to the dead. . . .

Thus was it made known that our Redeemer spent his time during his sojourn in the world of spirits, instructing and preparing the faithful spirits of the prophets who had testified of him in the flesh; that they might carry the message of redemption unto all the dead, unto whom he could not go personally, because of their rebellion and transgression, that they through the ministration of his servants might also hear his words. . . .

I beheld that the faithful elders of this dispensation, when they depart from mortal life, continue their labors in the preaching of the gospel of repentance and redemption, through the sacrifice of the Only Begotten Son of God, among those who are in darkness and under the bondage of sin in the great world of the spirits of the dead. . . .

Thus was the vision of the redemption of the dead revealed to me, and I bear record, and I know that this record is true, through the blessing of our Lord and Savior, Jesus Christ, even so. Amen.

—*Doctrine and Covenants 138:11–14, 18–20, 22–30, 36–37, 57, 60.*

Chapter 7

HEBER J. GRANT

Born: 22 November 1856
Ordained an Apostle: 16 October 1882
Ordained President: 23 November 1918
Died: 14 May 1945

ON THE RIGHT HAND. Every human being except those that have a knowledge of Jesus Christ and who sin against that knowledge, shall be saved; and in this revelation the wonderful testimony has been borne to us by the Prophet Joseph Smith and Sidney Rigdon:

"For we saw him, even on the right hand of God, and we heard the voice bearing record that he is the only begotten of the Father—

"That by him and through him, and of him, the worlds are and were created, and the inhabitants thereof are begotten sons and daughters unto God."

I bear witness to you, although I have not seen the Savior

sitting upon the right hand of God, I know that He lives; that
I know that Jesus is the Christ; that I know that Joseph Smith
was a prophet of God; I know that the signs follow the believer;
I know that hands are laid upon the sick and that the sick do
recover; I know that we have the gift of tongues among the
Latter-day Saints; I know that we have visions, dreams, and
revelations.
    —In Conference Report, April 1899, pp. 28–29.

LIGHT OF THE WORLD. I cannot understand how people
with a knowledge of the Gospel and the testimony that Jesus
is the Christ, that Joseph Smith was a Prophet of the true and
living God, and that he has established on the earth, under
the direction of our heavenly Father and his Son Jesus, the
Gospel of everlasting life, and that it is in very deed the pearl
of great price to each and every one of us—[and] that men,
holding the holy Priesthood and possessing this knowledge,
should, year after year, neglect the duties and the obligations
that rest upon them. The Savior told His followers that they
were the salt of the earth, but that if the salt lost its savor,
it was thenceforth good for nothing, but to be cast out and
trodden under the feet of men. He told them also that they
were the light of the world, a city set upon a hill which could
not be hid; he told them that men did not light a candle and
put it under a bushel, but upon a candlestick, that it might
give light to all that were in the room, and he admonished
them to let their light so shine that men seeing their good
deeds might glorify God.

    This admonition applies to us. We are the light of the
world. We have received the inspiration of Almighty God.
We have received a testimony of the Gospel, and we do know
that God lives, that Jesus is the Christ, that Joseph Smith
was a Prophet of God, and that Brigham Young, John Taylor,
and Wilford Woodruff were prophets of God, as is Lorenzo

Snow. Every true Latter-day Saint has this testimony burning
within his or her heart. Now, are we so living that the good
deeds we perform bring credit to the work of God? Are our
examples worthy of the imitation of all men? Do we by our
examples show that we have faith in the Gospel? We are told
that faith without works is dead; that as the body without the
spirit is dead, so also is faith without works dead, and I am
sorry to say that there are many professed Latter-day Saints
who are spiritually dead. We many times ask ourselves the
question, why does this man progress in the plan of life and
salvation, while his neighbor, of equal intelligence and ability,
of apparently the same testimony and power, and perchance
greater power, stands still? I will tell you why. One keeps the
commandments of our Heavenly Father, and the other fails
to keep them. The Savior says that he that keeps his commandments is the man that loves him, and he that keeps the
commandments of God shall be loved of the Father, and the
Savior says he will love him and he will manifest himself unto
him. The Lord also tells us that those who hear His sayings
and doeth them shall be likened unto the wise man who built
his house upon the rock, and when the rains descended and
the floods came and the winds blew and beat upon that house,
it fell not, because it was founded upon a rock. . . .

I have met many young men who have said to me, "I do
not know that the Gospel is true. I believe it, but I do not
know it." I have invariably replied to them that our Lord and
Master has said that he who will do the will of the Father
shall know of the doctrine, whether it be of God, or whether
he spoke of himself, and if they would do the will of the
Father, they should eventually have a knowledge of the Gospel. Some of them have said: "Oh, if I could only see an
angel; if I could only hear speaking in tongues; if I could only
see some great manifestation, then I would believe." I wish
to say to all within the sound of my voice that the seeing of

angels and great manifestations do not make great men in the Church and kingdom of God. Think of the three witnesses to the Book of Mormon. What is their testimony? It is that an angel showed them the plates, and that they knew they had been translated by the gift and power of God. How did they claim to know this? Because "His voice hath declared it unto us . . . an angel of God came down from heaven . . . we beheld and saw the plates, and the engravings thereon . . . the Lord commanded us that we should bear record of it. . . . " Yet these men fell by the wayside, though they remained true and steadfast to their testimony of the Book of Mormon. . . .

Think of it, beholding the glory of the Son and receiving a fullness of that glory, and hearing the voice declare that he is the only Begotten of the Father, and yet this man, Sidney Rigdon, proved a traitor to the Prophet and fell by the wayside! . . .

So it has been in all ages of the world, and so it will be with those who do not keep the commandments of God. Angels may visit them, they may see visions, they may have dreams, they may even see the Son of God, and yet the Spirit of God will not burn in their hearts. But those who do the will of God, and live God-like lives, they will grow and increase in the testimony of the Gospel and in power and ability to do God's will.

—In Conference Report, April 1900, pp. 21–23.

TESTIFYING BRINGS JOY. To me, one of the greatest testimonies of the divinity of the mission of our Savior is the joy and happiness that we all experience whenever we testify that He was in very deed the Son of God and the Redeemer of the world. I know of nothing that brings greater joy, except testifying regarding the divinity of the mission of the Savior than to testify regarding the divinity of the mission of the Prophet Joseph Smith.

The three years that I presided over the European mission were in very deed the most pleasurable, the most happy, the most satisfactory years of all my life. When instructing the Elders I told them whenever they seemed to be closed up in their spirits, whenever they seemed to lack ideas to express to the people, if they would only testify that they knew that Jesus was the Redeemer, and then testify regarding the divine mission of the Prophet Joseph Smith, that the Lord would open their mouths and bless them in speaking to the people. . . .

There is but one path of safety to the Latter-day Saints, and that is the path of duty. It is not a testimony, it is not marvelous manifestations, it is not knowing that the Gospel of Jesus Christ is true, that it is the plan of salvation, it is not actually knowing that the Savior is the Redeemer, and that Joseph Smith was His prophet, that will save you and me, but it is the keeping of the commandments of God, the living the life of a Latter-day Saint.

I have been profoundly impressed upon many occasions, as I have studied the history of the early men in this church, with the fact that one-half of the first quorum of Apostles fell by the wayside; that all of the three witnesses to the Book of Mormon, who saw the angel, who heard the voice of God, who heard the Lord testify to them that this work had been translated by the gift and power of God, that the Lord Himself, by His voice from heaven, had told these men to bear witness of this fact—should also fall by the wayside. The same with a majority of the eight witnesses. Oliver Cowdery, who heard the Savior's voice, and beheld a heavenly messenger before the Church was organized, gave a description, which is recorded in the Pearl of Great Price, of his ordination, in connection with the Prophet, to the Aaronic Priesthood, stating it was beyond the language of man to paint the joy and the grandeur that surrounded them upon that occasion. He also had the Apostles of the Lord Jesus Christ, who lived upon the earth in the days of our Savior, lay their hands upon his head and ordain him to the Melchizedek, or the Higher Priesthood. In the Kirtland Temple, with the Prophet Joseph Smith, he saw the Savior, also Moses, Elias, and Elijah. He had given to him, in connection with the Prophet, every key and every authority of all the dispensations of the Gospel of Jesus Christ, from the earliest time down to the present, and yet by failing to do his duty by failing to keep the commandments of God, this man lost his standing in the Church of Christ. True, he repented and came back. The same is true of Martin Harris. . . .

There is not a Latter-day Saint living who is keeping the commandments of the Lord, who would not regard it as one of the greatest joys imaginable if he could testify that he had heard the voice of God, and that the Lord had given him a commandment; and that, in fulfilment of the requirement of the Lord, he had recorded in this testimony: "we bear witness of these things." How we all would rejoice to be able to bear such a testimony; provided we had the Spirit of God; provided we were so living that it was not a dead letter with us.

—*In Conference Report, April 1915, pp. 82–83.*

I HAD BEEN INSPIRED OF THE LORD. I remember what to me was the greatest of all the great incidents in my life, in this tabernacle. I saw for the first time, in the audience, my brother who had been careless, indifferent and wayward, who had evinced no interest in the gospel of Jesus Christ, and, as I saw him for the first time in this building, and as I realized that he was seeking God for light and knowledge regarding the divinity of this work, I bowed my head and I prayed God that if I were requested to address the audience, that the Lord would inspire me by the revelations of his Spirit, by that Holy Spirit in whom every true Latter-day Saint believes, that my brother would have to acknowledge to me that I had spoken beyond my natural ability, that I had been inspired of the Lord. I realized that if he made that confession, then I should be able to point out to him that God had given him a testimony of the divinity of this work. Brother Milton Bennion was sitting on the stand that day, and he had been asked to address the congregation. President Angus M. Cannon came to me and said, "Before you entered the building, Brother Grant, I had invited Brother Milton Bennion to speak, but he can come some other day."

I said, "Let him speak." Brother Cannon said, "Well, I will ask him to speak briefly, and you will please follow him."

Brother Bennion told of his visit around the world; among other things, of visiting the sepulchre of Jesus.

I took out of my pocket a book that I always carried, called a *Ready Reference,* and I laid it down on the stand in front of me, when I stood up to speak. It was opened at the passages that tell of the vicarious work for the dead, of the announcement that Jesus went and preached to the spirits in prison, and proclaimed the gospel of Jesus Christ to them. . . .

I remember standing here feeling that was perhaps the greatest of all the great themes that we as Latter-day Saints had to proclaim to the world. I laid the book down, opened at that page; I prayed for the inspiration of the Lord, and the faith of the Latter-day Saints, and I never thought of the book from that minute until I sat down, at the end of a thirty-minute address. I closed my remarks . . . expecting that President George Q. Cannon would follow me. . . .

He arose and said in substance: "There are times when the Lord Almighty inspires some speaker by the revelations of his Spirit, and he is so abundantly blessed by the inspiration of the living God that it is a mistake for anybody else to speak following him, and one of those occasions has been today, and I desire that this meeting be dismissed without further remarks," and he sat down.

I devoted the thirty minutes of my speech almost exclusively to a testimony of my knowledge that God lives, that Jesus is the Christ, and to the wonderful and marvelous labors of the Prophet Joseph Smith, and bearing witness to the knowledge God had given me that Joseph was in very deed a prophet of the true and living God.

The next morning my brother came into my office and said, "Heber, I was at meeting yesterday and heard you preach."

I said, "The first time you ever heard your brother preach, I guess?"

"Oh, no," he said, "I have heard you lots of times."

I said, "I never saw you in meeting before."

"No," he said, "I generally come in late and go into the gallery. I often go out before the meeting is over. But you never spoke as you did yesterday. You spoke beyond your natural ability. You were inspired of the Lord." The identical words I had uttered the day before, in my prayer to the Lord. . . .

I answered, "And I was inspired beyond my natural ability; and I never spoke before—at any time you have heard me, as I spoke yesterday. Do you expect the Lord to get a club and knock you down? What more testimony do you want of the gospel of Jesus Christ than that a man speaks beyond his natural ability and under the inspiration of God, when he testifies of the divine mission of the prophet Joseph?" The next Sabbath he applied to me for baptism.

—In Conference Report, October 1922, pp.188–90.

ABSOLUTE FAITH IN JESUS CHRIST. As I travel I find a lack of belief in God, and in the divinity of Jesus Christ, even among the ministers of the gospel, I rejoice in the fact

that every man and woman in the Church of Jesus Christ of
Latter-day Saints has an absolute faith in God, in his individuality, and an absolute faith that Christ is the Son
of God, the Redeemer of the world; that he came to the earth
with a divinely appointed mission to die for the sins of the
world, and that he is in very deed the head of the Church of
Christ. . . .

I cut from a newspaper a clipping. . . . It was a recom-
mendation by an English lord that people discard the "ab-
surdity" of Jesus Christ as a God on earth and a Redeemer of
the world, and that they accept the Mohammedan philosophy;
suggesting that they could believe in all of the ethical teachings
of the religion of Christ and Mohammed, but that they should
get away from the absurdities of Christianity, and settle the
various disputes and troubles that they were having in the
Christian religion.

Wherever I read that statement . . . I took the trouble to
state to the people in the various places where I preached,
the position of the Latter-day Saints as to the gospel in which
we believe. I quoted the vision of Joseph Smith and Sidney
Rigdon, as follows:

"And this is the gospel, the glad tidings, which the voice
out of the heavens bore record unto us —

"That he came unto the world, even Jesus, to be crucified
for the world, and to bear the sins of the world, and to sanctify
the world, and to cleanse it from all unrighteousness;

"That through him all might be saved whom the Father
had put into his power and made by him;

"Who glorifies the Father, and saves all the works of his
hands, except those sons of perdition who deny the Son after
the Father has revealed him."

I announced to the people that in the Church of Jesus
Christ no man or woman would be admitted into the Church,
or be permitted to retain fellowship who is not willing to

accept this statement absolutely without mental reservation. . . .

I announced in those meetings, in some of which the
majority of the audience were non-members of the Church,
that every Latter-day Saint must subscribe to the doctrine that
God himself visited the boy Joseph Smith, and that God
himself introduced Jesus Christ to the boy as his well-beloved
Son. I announced to these audiences that among the Latter-
day Saints there is no evidence of "modernism" so-called, and
that no man or woman will be fellowshiped in this Church
who denies the individuality, the personality of God, or that
Jesus Christ is in very deed the Son of the living God, the
Redeemer of the world.

—In Conference Report, April 1925, pp. 7–8.

POWER OF CHRIST. When I was a young unmarried man,
another young man who had received a doctor's degree ridiculed me for believing in the Book of Mormon. [A] . . .
statement that this doctor made was this: that the voice of
man can only carry a few hundred feet, and yet the Book of
Mormon teaches that when Jesus Christ was resurrected and
came to this country he spoke to the people and his voice was
heard all over the land, not alone by the people that were
near, but all over the land. "That is a lie," said he, "and you
know it." I said, "That is no lie at all. Jesus Christ, under
God, was the Creator of this earth, and if he had the power
and ability to create the earth I believe that he could arrange
for his voice to carry all over the world at one and the same
time."

—In Conference Report, April 1929, pp. 129–30.

PROVE TO THE LORD BY OUR LIVES. God help you
and me and every Latter-day Saint to prove to the Lord by
our lives, that our testimony of the divinity of this work is

not merely lip service. . . . God bless every man that believes in Jesus Christ and is working for the uplift of mankind, and God defeat every man who ridicules the Savior of the world, the Redeemer of mankind.
—In Conference Report, October 1934, p. 132.

THE FATHER OF CHRIST. When we say that we believe in God we mean that we believe in him as an individuality, as actually the Father of Jesus Christ—not a congeries of laws floating through the universe without form and void, but we believe him to be the Father of Jesus Christ. He is the God whom we as Latter-day Saints worship; and we believe Jesus Christ to be, not only one of the great moral teachers, the greatest the world has ever known, but the Son of God, the Redeemer of mankind, that he came to earth with a divinely appointed mission, to die on the cross, in order that you and I and all eventually may have part in the resurrection.
—In Conference Report, April 1935, p. 10.

GOD AND JESUS CHRIST DID COME. I have met hundreds of men who have said, "If it were not for Joseph Smith I could accept your religion." Any man who does not believe in Joseph Smith as a prophet of the true and the living God has no right to be in this Church. That revelation to Joseph Smith is the foundation stone. If Joseph Smith did not have that interview with God and Jesus Christ the whole Mormon fabric is a failure and a fraud. It is not worth anything on earth. But God did come, God did introduce his Son, God did inspire that man to organize the Church of Jesus Christ, and all the opposition of the world is not able to withstand the truth. It is flourishing, it is growing, and it will grow more.
—In Conference Report, October 1939, p. 128.

WE BELIEVE IN GOD. A gentleman sent out several

hundred letters to representative ministers, and asked them the question: "Do you believe in God, a personal God, a definite and tangible intelligence, not a congeries of laws floating like a fog in the universe, but God a person, in whose image you were made?" Not a minister answered , "yes." They said they could not be certain about a thing of that kind. . . .

We declare to all the world that God lives, that He is the Father of our spirits, that He is absolutely the Father of Jesus Christ, that Jesus Christ is the Redeemer of the world. Men say we lack liberality and breadth, because we say we are the only true Church. We are not lacking in liberality or breadth; the Redeemer of the world, Jesus Christ, our Lord and Savior, said it, and we are repeating what He said.

—*In Conference Report, April 1922, pp. 11–12.*

THE LORD MAKES NO MISTAKES. It has never ceased to be a wonder to me that I do represent the Lord here upon the earth. My association from childhood with the remarkable and wonderful men that have preceded me has made it almost overwhelming to think of being in the same class with them.

The last words uttered by President Joseph F. Smith were to the effect, when he shook hands with me—he died that night—"The Lord bless you, my boy, the Lord bless you; you have got a great responsibility. Always remember this is the Lord's work and not man's. The Lord is greater than any man. He knows whom he wants to lead His Church, and never makes any mistake. The Lord bless you."

I have felt my own lack of ability. In fact when I was called as one of the Apostles I arose to my feet to say it was beyond anything I was worthy of, and as I was rising the thought came to me, "You know as you know that you live that John Taylor is a prophet of God, and to decline this office when he had received a revelation is equivalent to repudiating the Prophet." I said, "I will accept the office and do my best."

I remember that it was with difficulty that I took my seat without fainting.

There are two spirits striving with us always, one telling us to continue our labor for good, and one telling us that with the faults and failings of our nature we are unworthy. I can truthfully say that from October, 1882, until February, 1883, that spirit followed me day and night telling me that I was unworthy to be an Apostle of the Church, and that I ought to resign. When I would testify of my knowledge that Jesus is the Christ, the Son of the Living God, the Redeemer of mankind, it seemed as though a voice would say to me: "You lie! You lie! You have never seen Him."

While on the Navajo Indian reservation with Brigham Young, Jr., and a number of others, six or eight, on horseback, and several others in "white tops"—riding along with Lot Smith at the rear of that procession, suddenly the road veered to the left almost straight, but there was a well beaten path leading ahead. I said: "Stop, Lot, stop. Where does this trail lead? There are plenty of foot marks and plenty of horses' hoof marks here." He said, "It leads to an immense gully just a short distance ahead, that is impossible to cross with a wagon. We have made a regular 'Muleshoe' of miles here to get on the other side of the gully."

I had visited the day before the spot where a Navajo Indian had asked George A. Smith, Jr., to let him look at his pistol. George A. handed it to him, and the Navajo shot him.

I said, "Lot, is there any danger from Indians?"

"None at all."

"I want to be all alone. Go ahead and follow the crowd." I first asked him if I allowed the animal I was riding to walk if I would reach the road on the other side of the gully before the horsemen and the wagons, and he said, "Yes."

As I was riding along to meet them on the other side I seemed to see, and I seemed to hear, what to me is one of

the most real things in all my life, I seemed to see a Council
in Heaven. I seemed to hear the words that were spoken. I
listened to the discussion with a great deal of interest. The
First Presidency and the Council of the Twelve Apostles had
not been able to agree on two men to fill the vacancies in
the Quorum of the Twelve. There had been a vacancy of one
for two years, a vacancy of two for one year, and the Conference had adjourned without the vacancies being filled. In
this Council the Savior was present, my father was there, and
the Prophet Joseph Smith was there. They discussed the question that a mistake had been made in not filling those two
vacancies and that in all probability it would be another six
months before the Quorum would be completed, and they
discussed as to whom they wanted to occupy those positions,
and decided that the way to remedy the mistake that had been
made in not filling these vacancies was to send a revelation.
It was given to me that the Prophet Joseph Smith and my
father mentioned me and requested that I be called to that
position. I sat there and wept for joy. It was given to me that
I had done nothing to entitle me to that exalted position,
except that I had lived a clean, sweet life. It was given to me
that because of my father having practically sacrificed his life
in what was known as the great Reformation, so to speak, of
the people in early days, having been practically a martyr,
that the Prophet Joseph and my father desired me to have
that position, and it was because of their faithful labors that
I was called, and not because of anything I had done of myself
or any great thing that I had accomplished. It was also given
to me that that was all these men, the Prophet and my father,
could do for me; from that day it depended upon me and upon
me alone as to whether I made a success of my life or a
failure. . . .

    I have been happy during the twenty-two years that it has
fallen my lot to stand at the head of this Church. I have felt

the inspiration of the Living God directing me in my labors. From the day that I chose a comparative stranger to be one of the Apostles, instead of my lifelong and dearest living friend, I have known as I know that I live, that I am entitled to the light and the inspiration and the guidance of God in directing His work here upon this earth; and I know, as I know that I live, that it is God's work, and that Jesus Christ is the Son of the Living God, the Redeemer of the world and that He came to this earth with a divine mission to die upon the cross as the Redeemer of mankind, atoning for the sins of the world.

   —In *Conference Report*, April 1941, pp. 4–6.

GREATER THE JOY. It is a remarkable fact that we can never read of the labors which [Jesus Christ] performed, or listen to others speaking of the great work which he accomplished, without taking pleasure in it, while on the other hand, there is nothing so interesting in the life and history of any other individual but what by hearing and reading it time and time again we become tired of it. I can bear testimony, from my own experience, that the oftener I read of the life and labors of our Lord and Savior Jesus Christ the greater are the joy, the peace, the happiness, the satisfaction that fill my soul in contemplating what he did.

   —In *Conference Report*, April 1944, p. 7.

Chapter 8

GEORGE ALBERT SMITH

Born: 4 April 1870
Ordained an Apostle: 8 October 1903
Ordained President: 21 May 1945
Died: 4 April 1951

A PARALLEL BETWEEN JESUS CHRIST AND JOSEPH SMITH. When our Savior in humility came upon earth, the people said, "Who are you, that you should claim to be the Son of God? We know your father; he is Joseph, the carpenter. We know your mother; she is Mary. We have Moses and Abraham for our prophets, and we have no need of a man like you to come and speak to us in the name of the Lord." He went among them and ministered to the sick, healed the afflicted, unstopped the ears of the deaf, restored the blind to sight, cleansed the leper by His magic touch, raised the dead to life. Then they said He performed these wondrous works by the power of Beelzebub. Yet He was indeed the Son of

God. He labored among them in love and kindness; but they cast His name out as evil. They even cast reproach upon the city from which He came, and said, "Can any good thing come out of Nazareth?" But He was the Son of God, and He did have the right to speak in the name of the Father. The truths He brought to the earth came from the Father; and though they nailed Him to the cross, though they placed upon His head the plaited crown of thorns, and put the mock scepter in His hands, though they spilled His blood with the cruel spear, yet the word that He delivered to them was the word of the Lord, and He was indeed the Son of God.

The same feeling that was entertained, to some extent, against the Savior has continued in the earth. People who do not understand the things of God because they have not the Spirit of God, reviled and cast them out as evil, when in fact the evil is in themselves. . . .

Our Heavenly Father . . . chose and commissioned Joseph Smith, as He had done other prophets, to go forth among the people and speak in the name of the Lord. Through this humble instrument, the Gospel was restored to the earth again and he preached the same doctrines that our Savior taught while He was upon the earth. Under the Lord's direction, he organized the Church of Christ, with apostles, prophets, pastors, teachers, evangelists, etc., as the Church should be organized, to continue thus until all should come to a unity of the faith. He ministered unto the people, he healed the sick; he loved the souls of the children of men. But, as had been the case with prophets whom the Lord had raised up before, it seemed necessary in this case that the testimony of His servant should be sealed with his life's blood. . . . You remember when he was first raised up how the people of this country said, "We have no need of you. You are Joseph, the son of Joseph, and we know where you come from. You are not a strong and mighty man, and you do not come from an influential family. We have no need of new revelation. We have the Bible, and that is all that is necessary for the salvation of the children of men. . . . The people of the world, as before, judge this work by the spirit of man. They do not have the Spirit of God, which would enable them to understand that it came from our Father in heaven.

— In Conference Report, April 1904, pp. 63–64.

JESUS CHRIST, OUR SAVIOR. I rejoice this day in a testimony of the divinity of the mission of Jesus Christ, the Redeemer of the world. I know, as I know that I live, that He is what we believe Him to be. I know that there is no other name under heaven whereby we may hope to gain exaltation, but the name of Jesus Christ, our Savior. There is no other Gospel of salvation, and we, my brethren who bear the holy priesthood, have the responsibility of carrying that message, not only to the nations of the earth, but of exemplifying it in our lives and teaching it to those who are our neighbors, not of our faith. I warn you this day that the Lord holds us responsible to call His children to repentance and for the promulgation of His truth. If we fail to take advantage of our opportunities to teach the sons and daughters of God, who are not of our faith, who dwell in our midst, this Gospel of our Lord, He will require at our hands on the other side of the veil what we have failed to do, so let us not be recreant.

— In Conference Report, April 1916, p. 48.

YOUR SCHOOL MASTER. You have had the greatest instructor that the world knows anything about. You have had for your school master the King of kings, the Lord of lords, the Creator of the heavens and the earth; who in his wonderful tenderness and consideration for us in this day, has sent his prophet into the world to explain to us, and to make clear to our minds the things that he gave to the world hundreds of

years ago that have been misunderstood and have been mis-interpreted very much to the detriment of our Father's chil-dren. But in our day he has renewed to us the truth, has given to us the blessed teachings that should qualify us to be men and women after his own heart, has held out to us the promise that if we will do the things that he advises our lives will be pure and holy, peace will be our portion here, and we shall dwell with him throughout the ages of eternity. What more could he give unto us, or, . . . "What more can he say than to you he has said, you who unto Jesus for refuge have fled?"
    —In Conference Report, October 1923, p. 73.

To Be Taught by the Lord. How grateful we ought to be that there has been removed from us the doubt that exists in the minds of so many of our Father's splendid sons and daughters, that there has come to us that abiding assurance that God lives, that Jesus is the Christ, that he is our elder brother, and that if we are faithful, in his own due time he will cleanse and purify this earth on which we dwell, and it will be celestialized, and those who have prepared themselves for the celestial kingdom will have the joy of dwelling hereon, to be directed, to be counseled, to be taught, and advised by the Lord of lords and King of kings, throughout the ages of eternity. What a wonderful promise . . . has been given to the children of men, and oh, how I pray that there may come into the souls of the thousands and millions of God's children a knowledge of the purpose of their being, that they may prepare, while there is yet time before their final summons, for the time when we will be classified and placed in whatever kingdom we have earned the right to dwell in, when we go to the other side.
    —In Conference Report, October 1925, pp. 33–34.

No Other Name in Heaven. Above all, I thank him

for the knowledge that has been burned into my soul; I know that my heavenly Father lives, I know that Jesus Christ is the Savior of mankind, and that there is no other name under heaven whereby men and women may be exalted, but the name of Jesus Christ, our Lord. I do know that he came into the world in this latter day, that he bestowed divine authority upon a humble boy who was seeking the truth, and the result of that has been the organization of the Church with which we are identified; and there is with it the power of God unto salvation to all those who believe.

—In Conference Report, October 1927, p. 50.

TRUE PORTRAIT OF CHRIST. Christ, the ideal, has been falsely portrayed so much by word and brush that he is thought of as being weak, and effeminate; whereas, he was vigorous, active, and courageous. The basis of his doctrine was individual responsibility, which calls forth the best and most virile attributes of man.

—Improvement Era, 31 (1927-28): 689.

THE LORD SPEAKS THROUGH PROPHETS. One of the prophets told us that the Lord God would do nothing but He would reveal His secrets to His servants the prophets. In other words, the world would not be taken by surprise if they paid attention to the leadership that the Lord provided. So we look down over the vista of time, to the days of Noah when the Lord warned the people of what would occur, and they apparently paid no attention, for out of the seeming multitudes that dwelt upon the earth, only eight souls were saved from destruction, yet all had been told how they might be preserved.

The Lord warned Tyre and Nineveh and Jerusalem and Babylon, and other cities, that unless they repented and turned to him they would be destroyed, and of those cities, Nineveh was the only one that turned immediately to the Lord. . . .

The Lord told Abraham that his seed should go into a strange land, that after four hundred years they would return with great possessions. . . .

Think how anxious the Lord was to save the cities of the plains, Sodom and Gomorrah. Abraham pleaded repeatedly with the Lord, asking that they be spared for the sake of the righteous. He kept reducing the number until he came down from fifty to ten righteous people. The Lord said that if in these cities ten righteous could be found, the cities would be saved. But not ten righteous persons could be found and the cities were destroyed. . . .

It was a strange thing that in the days of Isaiah the Lord revealed to him that the greatest of all the nations in the earth should be humbled. . . .

It was not very long after that until the Jews who would not repent were punished because they would not listen to the Lord. And then again, after the coming of our Lord and Master, Jesus Christ, they would not receive His Gospel and they would not repent. This time Jerusalem was not only overthrown but was destroyed and her temple was razed until not one stone was left upon another.

All these things were revealed to the prophets of God. And so we might go on now speaking of Babylon, and how the Lord told of the establishment of the various kingdoms that should succeed, by giving the king, Nebuchadnezzar, a dream, and then by using Daniel, who was there as a captive to interpret the dream of the king. The prediction had been made that certain things would occur, and one kingdom should follow after another, and it was so fulfilled. It took hundreds of years to fulfil the prediction. . . .

In the year 1830 he established His Church here upon the earth. That did not come by accident — it did not come by surprise. It had all been predicted — all these things that are contained in the Old and New Testaments. . . . I am trying to call your attention to the fact that when the Lord speaks, what He promises has always been fulfilled.

Well, now, has He promised us anything today? Read your scriptures. Not only the Old and New Testaments, but turn to your Book of Mormon. See how the Lord has fulfilled His promises — how the Nephites, because they refused to accept the teachings of God — refused to sustain those who presided over them by authority — were wiped from the face of the earth. That was not done without a warning; they knew it would come, and they were told, across the mighty ocean, of the coming of the Savior, what would occur when He came, and what would happen when He was crucified. . . .

You may follow the record, and you will discover that such things have never happened to a people who were keeping the commandments of God. The destruction has come to those who were failing to pay attention to what the Lord desired. This nation was raised up in order that men might worship God according to the dictates of their conscience — this nation of which we are a part. God raised up the very men who prepared the Constitution to declare to us our privileges and our liberties. It was not an accident. Those things were re-corded beforehand. In the Book of Mormon He announced the coming of Columbus, and of the Pilgrim fathers, from the old world, those who came here to worship God.

All these things had been made known beforehand, and then, in the case of the Latter-day Saints when they were in distress in Nauvoo and were being harassed by their enemies, the Prophet of God told them that they would be driven from their homes — and that they would come to the tops of the Rocky Mountains where they would become a mighty people. What did they know about the Rocky Mountains? What was there in the Rocky Mountains that they should come to? Not anything but what God had prepared. That prophecy was fulfilled, and you are my witnesses that it was fulfilled in that the Latter-day Saints today are a mighty people in the midst of these great mountain valleys.

Another prediction of our times that was fulfilled, was when the Lord revealed to the Prophet Joseph Smith that there would be a civil war in this country and told him exactly where it would begin, at the rebellion of South Carolina. How did the Prophet Joseph know, nearly thirty years before it occurred, that it would start in South Carolina? He knew because the Lord knew and told him so. So from the beginning, through Noah, and all down through the line of prophets the power to communicate with the heavens has been with those whom God has raised up and prepared. The people have been taught, and they have been warned, and most of them have been recreant to the warning, the result being that great destruction has come upon the children of men.

—In Conference Report, October 1943, pp. 43–44.

THE CHURCH OF JESUS CHRIST. We have the peculiar distinction of belonging to a Church that does not have the name of any man, because it was not organized by the wisdom of any man. It was named by the Father of us all in honor of his Beloved Son, Jesus Christ.

I would like to suggest to you . . . that we honor the name of the Church. It is not the Church of James and John, it is not the church of Moroni, nor is it the church of Mormon. It is the Church of Jesus Christ. And while all these men were wonderful and notable characters, we have been directed to worship God in a church that bears the name of his Beloved Son. . . .

When Christ came to instruct the people, he told them that there must be faith in God and righteousness in life or they would not please our Heavenly Father. And so the Savior of the world came with kindness and love. He went among the people healing the sick, unstopping the ears of the deaf, and restoring sight to those who were blind. They saw these things done by the power of God. Comparatively few of them could understand or believe that he was the Son of God. . . .

His only Begotten Son in the flesh had to call the attention of his associates to the fact that with all his majesty and his royalty, he still must live like other men. And when the time came for him to die, and be hung upon the cross, and cruelly tortured by those of his own people, his own race, he did not become angry, he did not resent the unkindness.

When the one thief on the cross railed against him, the other thief called attention to the fact that they were only receiving their just desserts, while here was a righteous man being unjustly punished. The one thief prayed, as best he knew how to pray, and the Savior of the World said to this man who was suspended alongside him on another cross:

" . . . To day shalt thou be with me in paradise." (Luke 23:43.)

The people of the world do not understand some of these things, and particularly, many men cannot understand how the Savior felt when in the agony of his soul, he cried to his Heavenly Father, not to condemn and destroy these who were taking his mortal life, but he said:

" . . . Father, forgive them; for they know not what they do." (Luke 23:34.)

That should be the attitude of all the members of The Church of Jesus Christ of Latter-day Saints. That should be the attitude of all the sons and daughters of God and would be, it seems to me, if they fully understood the plan of salvation. . . . So it is our privilege, possessing divine authority that has been conferred again in our day, to go into the world and teach men the message of the Savior that would have redeemed the world if people had accepted it.

— In Conference Report, October 1945, pp. 167–69.

LIVE THE TEACHINGS OF JESUS. If we will live the teachings of Jesus of Nazareth, if we will observe the advice and counsel of the prophets of God, if we will carry out the program that the Lord has given to the Church with which we are identified, we will lead all the world in knowledge and intelligence and in power, because we may have all that the world has, plus the inspiration of the Almighty.
—In Conference Report, April 1946, p. 124.

KNOWLEDGE OF GOD. This poor old world today would not be in the condition it is in if the people who live on it believed in God, the Eternal Father, and in His Son, Jesus Christ, and in the Holy Ghost. People talk about believing, but two-thirds of those who live on this earth know practically nothing at all about the God of Abraham, Isaac and Jacob. Of the other one-third, the so-called Christians, about fifty per cent know very little about the personality of God, and know very little about being here for any particular reason; they are just here. They are something like Topsy. When they asked her where she came from, she said she didn't know, —she just growed. It is a wonderful thing to have the privilege that all other people of the world have, every opportunity to obtain education and culture, and besides, that which is more important than all the rest, to have a knowledge that God is our Father, that we are His children, and that Jesus Christ is His Son, our elder Brother. The world does not understand what it all means. . . .

I know that God lives, I know that Jesus is the Christ, I know that Joseph Smith was and is a prophet of the living God, that the Gospel of our Lord is here on earth and we have the opportunity to conform our lives to its principles and be blessed thereby.

I realize that there are some who say, "I can't believe," but that does not change my knowledge of the truth. I know it just the same. I know another thing, that if I were not telling the truth in testifying as I do, I would have to account to my Heavenly Father for seeking to deceive. I am taking into account what it all means. I realize the seriousness of my testimony and here in the presence of all of you I leave that witness.

—28 April 1946 address at graduation exercises, Wasatch LDS Seminary, Heber City, Utah, LDS Church Archives.

SERIOUSNESS OF TESTIMONY. We are not out of the woods. This world is in for a housecleaning unless the sons and daughters of our Heavenly Father repent of their sins and turn to him. And that means the Latter-day Saints, or members of the Church of Jesus Christ of Latter-day Saints, along with all the rest, but we, first of all, ought to be setting the example. . . . I know that God lives. I know that Jesus is the Christ. I know that Joseph Smith was a Prophet of the Living God, and had restored to him the true gospel of Jesus Christ in these latter days.

That might sound like boasting if it were not so serious. It is serious, and I know that I will have to answer for that testimony as I leave it with you. . . . It will not be long until this man who is talking will have finished his work and passed to the other side, and when I go, I want to be worthy to join my grandparents and my parents, my brothers and sisters who have passed on. I know they have earned a place that is worth while. I want to go where they have gone, and I know that if I were not to tell you the truth in regard to this matter, I might lose that opportunity.

So, realizing the seriousness of a testimony like that, realizing what it means, and with love unfeigned and a desire to be a blessing to all our Father's children, I leave this witness with you that this is the gospel of Jesus Christ, the only power of God unto salvation in preparation for the celestial kingdom, into which kingdom we may all go if we will, but it will be on his terms.

—In Conference Report, October 1946, p. 153.

BLESSINGS OF RIGHTEOUSNESS. Every blessing we enjoy is the result of keeping the commandments of God. Every blessing we desire we must obtain on those same terms. So today I witness to you that we have a Heavenly Father— I know that he lives. I know that Jesus was the Christ, his Beloved Son, who gave his mortal life that we might have eternal life. He came to this country twice, once to the Nephites, and later in the days of Joseph Smith. The Father and the Son came in that latter instance to see that the way was opened for the dissemination of his gospel. He has called us to bear the priesthood and carry the gospel message as missionaries to the various parts of the world, and in return for that he has promised us eternal life in his celestial kingdom.

—In Conference Report, April 1947, p. 166.

PART OF THE LORD'S WORK. We are thankful to him who is the Author of our being, and grateful that he came down to earth and brought with him his Beloved Son to begin a new dispensation—the Dispensation of the Fullness of Times. This is not the Church of Joseph Smith or of any other leader who followed him. This is the Church of Jesus Christ, and it was our Heavenly Father who gave it its name.

I wonder sometimes if we realize what an honor it is to have membership in this great organization. Even in our business affairs and in our social affairs we should carry with us the feeling, "I am a part of the work of the Lord, and I desire to be worthy of the blessings that have come to me." . . .

Some people have worshiped the sun; some have worshiped other luminaries; and some have worshiped mountains and other things, with the thought that it was worship. But the worship in the Church of Jesus Christ of Latter-day Saints is a devoted life, a desire to be worthy of him in whose image we have been created and who has given us all that the world has that is worth while — the gospel of Jesus Christ.

—In Conference Report, April 1949, pp. 7–8.

RESURRECTION OF THE REDEEMER. When we think of the resurrection of our Redeemer, I am reminded that the purpose of his life was to prepare us all, to make a path that we could all walk, that would bring us eternal happiness in his presence as well as in the presence of one another. He gave his life and testified by the shedding of his blood that he was a Son of God, and then . . . his appearance since that time has demonstrated beyond any possible doubt that he was what he claimed to be.

—In Conference Report, April 1950, p. 168.

OUR BELIEF AND WITNESSES OF CHRIST. I know of no people in the world who believe as firmly in the divine mission of Jesus Christ as do the membership of The Church of Jesus Christ of Latter-day Saints. I remember I have had many people say to me, "Why, you people do not even believe in Jesus Christ."

I have said, "What is the matter with you? If we do not believe in Jesus Christ, why do we call the Church, the Church of Jesus Christ?"

"Oh, I didn't know you called it that, I thought it was called the Mormon Church," they have replied. . . .

When people say or think that we do not believe in the divine mission of Jesus Christ, let them know that we believe all that the Bible teaches in reference to him. We believe the story of how he organized his people and taught them, and how eventually, at the insistence of his own people, he was crucified by the representatives of the Roman government;

not for any wrong he had done, but because he was too good to live among that people. . . .

We have all the information that our Christian brothers and sisters do with regard to the life of the Savior in the Bible, and in addition to that, we have the story of his coming to the people on this western hemisphere, as recorded in the Book of Mormon. And when he came among them, he talked to them as he had to those in the old world. When he was ready to leave them, he blessed them, he healed their sick and took their children up in his arms and wept over them. And after being with them two or three days, coming and going, they saw him ascend into heaven. . . .

We not only have all that the world has with regard to the divinity of the mission of Jesus Christ as recorded in the Bible, but also we have the story of another book, known as the Book of Mormon, and the account of his appearing in this western hemisphere . . . ; and we also have the story of another man who gave his life as a witness that he knew that God lives and Jesus is the Christ. I refer to the Prophet Joseph Smith. . . .

If men and women, with all the truth that they have, would retain all the wonderful things that have been passed on through the prophets of God, and then let us share with them the additional information the Lord has revealed since the Holy Bible was made accessible to the world, what a difference it would make.

—In Conference Report, October 1950, pp. 156–58.

ENJOYED HIS COMPANIONSHIP. I have been buoyed up and, as it were, lifted out of myself and given power not my own to teach the glorious truths proclaimed by the Redeemer of the world. I have not seen Him face to face but have enjoyed the companionship of His Spirit and felt His presence in a way not to be mistaken. I know that my Re-

deemer lives and gladly yield my humble efforts to establish
his teachings. The philosophies of men can never take the
place of truth as revealed to us by the Eternal Father. Individual
happiness and world-wide peace will not be permanent until
those who dwell in the earth accept the Gospel and conform
their lives to its precepts. . . . Every fibre of my being vibrates
with the knowledge that He lives and some day all men will
know it.

The Savior died that we might live. He overcame death
and the grave and holds out to all who obey His teachings
the hope of the glorious resurrection."

—*Forace Green, comp.,* Testimonies of Our Leaders *(Salt Lake City:*
Bookcraft, 1958), 53.

Chapter 9

DAVID O. McKAY

Born: 8 September 1873
Ordained an Apostle: 9 April 1906
Sustained as President: 9 April 1951
Died: 18 January 1970

RESISTING SATAN'S TEMPTATIONS. Latter-day Saints are members of the Church . . . for the developing of the religious sentiment, the true religious spirit. This may be done in two ways: first, by *seeking the truth,* and *living in harmony* with it; and second, by *resisting every influence, every power* that *tends to destroy or to dwarf in any way the religious sentiment.* . . .

Take as an example the Savior. After He passed through that ordinance to fulfill all righteousness, after He had received the commendation of the Father and the testimony from on high that He was the Son of God, the "Beloved Son" in whom the Father was well pleased, Satan was there ready to thwart

His mission. Jesus went forth in fasting and prayer, preparatory
for the great mission resting upon Him; and when in His
weakest moment—as Satan thought—when His body was
weak and exhausted by long fasting, the evil one presented
himself in temptation; and what was the temptation? An
appeal to His bodily weakness: "If thou be the Son of God—
(note the taunt—the very testimony on the bank of the Jordan
was, "This is my beloved Son;") "If thou be the Son of God,
command that these stones be made bread." In a moment of
weakness and hunger, that temptation would be strongest,
other things being equal. There was the moment of *resistance*
on Jesus' part. His *seeking* had been manifested in prayer and
fasting; His resistance came, at the moment of bodily weakness. Though the body was weak the Spirit was strong and
Christ answered: "It is written, man shall not live by bread
alone, but by every word that proceedeth out of the mouth
of God." Then Satan tried Him on another point. Failing in
that, the tempter tried Him still on the third, tempted Him
first on His love for physical comfort; second, tempted Him
on vanity, and third, tempted Him on love for worldly wealth,
and the power to rule the world. But all these temptations
Christ resisted; and the final resistance was: "Get thee behind
me Satan, for it is written: Thou shalt worship the Lord thy
God and Him only shalt thou serve." . . . This element of
resistance in regard to our bodily longings—satisfying the passions, applies to every member of the Church of Christ. In
some way the evil one will attack us. In some way he can
weaken us; in some way he will bring before us that which
will weaken our souls, and will tend to thwart that true development of religious sentiment; and what I mean by that is
this: the development of the spirit within, the strengthening
of the inner man, the strengthening and growth of the spirit,
that time cannot kill, but which is enduring and lasting as
the eternal Father of that spirit. And the things that will tend

to dwarf this spirit or to hinder its growth are things that the Latter-day Saints are called upon to resist.

—In Conference Report, April 1907, pp. 11–12.

VISION OF THOSE WHO HAVE OVERCOME THE WORLD. I then fell asleep, and beheld in vision something infinitely sublime. In the distance I beheld a beautiful white city. Though far away, yet I seemed to realize that trees with luscious fruit, shrubbery with gorgeously tinted leaves, and flowers in perfect bloom abounded everywhere. The clear sky above seemed to reflect these beautiful shades of color. I then saw a great concourse of people approaching the city. Each one wore a white flowing robe and a white headdress. Instantly my attention seemed centered upon their leader, and though I could see only the profile of his features and his body, I recognized him at once as my Savior. The tint and radiance of his countenance were glorious to behold. There was a peace about him which seemed sublime—it was divine!

The city, I understood, was his. It was the City Eternal; and the people following him were to abide there in peace and eternal happiness.

But who were they?

As if the Savior read my thoughts, he answered by pointing to a semicircle that then appeared above them, and on which were written in gold the words:

These Are They Who Have Overcome The World—
Who Have Truly Been Born Again!

—Experienced on ship while nearing Samoa, recorded in 10 May 1921 entry in David O. McKay's world tour diary, in Cherished Experiences from the Writings of David O. McKay, comp. Clare Middlemiss (Salt Lake City: Deseret Book Company, 1976), 59–60.

THE CHURCH FOUNDED UPON THE REALITY OF CHRIST. As the Christian church in the meridian of time was founded upon the reality of the living Christ—not merely upon the teachings of the Great Teacher—so the Church of Jesus Christ in this age was founded upon the reality of Christ's existence and upon the reality of his appearance in this dispensation to the earnest seeking boy, Joseph Smith.

—In Conference Report, April 1926, p. 39.

KEEP THE FAITH. What does it mean to keep the faith? It means first, that we accept Jesus Christ, not merely as a great teacher, a powerful leader, but as the Savior, the Redeemer of the world. . . . Many students are reading comments from reputably great educators who say that in order to be a christian it is not necessary to accept Christ as the literal Son of God, it is not necessary to believe in the immaculate conception, it is not necessary to believe in the literal resurrection from the grave. But he who keeps the faith will accept Jesus Christ as the Son of God, the Redeemer of the world. . . . A young man who keeps that faith may not in his heart know that all things which Jesus said are true, but if he holds to the truth of Christ's divinity he will keep in harmony with the Savior's teachings by the spirit of faith. And we walk by faith in this world. We are as the little boy who holds his father's hand in the midst of a great city: the little boy is confused by the din and bustle of the crowd, and realizes that if he breaks away he will be lost and may not be able to get back to his father. While he holds that father's hand, however, he is safe. He has an assurance that his father will lead him back to his home. So it is with the young man who keeps his faith in this latter-day work. There may be confusion around him, his thoughts may be distracted, but he has his hand in that of his Redeemer, and with faith in that spiritual inspiration he will be led into truth, his conscience will be awakened to that great spiritual reality which is around us.

—In Conference Report, October 1928, pp. 36–37.

ALWAYS REMEMBER HIM. The sacrament is a memorial of Christ's life and death. When we think of his life we think of sacrifice. Not a moment of his existence on earth did Christ think more of himself than he did of his brethren and the people whom he came to save, always losing himself for the good of others, and finally giving his life for the redemption of mankind. When we partake of the sacrament in his presence we remember him, his life of sacrifice, and service; and we are inspired by that thought and memory. There is nothing won in this life without sacrifice. . . .

The partaking of the sacrament indicates also how communion with Christ may be secured. It cannot be obtained by Sunday righteousness and week-day indulgence. It implies that we will remember Christ always.

—*In Conference Report, October 1929, pp. 11–13.*

MARK TESTIFIED OF CHRIST. We have no evidence that Mark joined the Church while the Savior was on the earth. Undoubtedly the Savior was in Mark's home. Mark was probably the youth who rushed into the garden of Gethsemane and warned Jesus that the soldiers were coming. At any rate we are justified in assuming that he was acquainted with the Master.

Mark does not himself recount any appearance of the risen Lord; but he testifies that the angel at the tomb announced the resurrection, and promised that the Lord would meet his disciples. From Mark we hear the glorious proclamation of the first empty tomb in all the world. For the first time in the history of man the words "Here lies" were supplanted by the divine message "He is risen." No one can doubt that Mark was not convinced in his soul of the reality of the empty tomb. To him the resurrection was not questionable—it was real; and the appearance of his Lord and Master among men was a fact established in his mind beyond the shadow of a doubt.

To the proclaiming of this truth he devoted his life, and if
tradition can be relied upon, he sealed his testimony with his
blood."
    —*In Conference Report, April 1939, p. 113.*

NEW PROPHET SPEAKS. When the Savior was about to
leave his Apostles, he gave them a great example of service.
You remember he girded himself with a towel and washed his
disciples' feet. . . .

    Returning the basin to the side of the door, ungirding
himself, and putting on his robe, he returned to his position
with the Twelve, and said:

    "Ye call me Master and Lord: and . . . so I am."

    What an example of service to those great servants, fol-
lowers of the Christ! He that is greatest among you, let him
be least. So we sense the obligation to be of greater service
to the membership of the Church, to devote our lives to the
advancement of the kingdom of God on earth.
    —*In Conference Report, April 1951, pp. 158–59.*

THE GREAT HIGH PRIEST. The Priesthood came direct
from our Lord and Savior, Jesus Christ, who is the great High
Priest, and he authorized Peter, James and John, on whom
he bestowed that Priesthood, to bestow it upon the Prophet
Joseph Smith; and John the Baptist, who held the Aaronic
Priesthood to bestow the Aaronic Priesthood upon Joseph
Smith. Joseph Smith did not take it; it came direct, and you
brethren . . . can trace your ordination, probably within five
steps, right back to the Savior himself.
    —*In Conference Report, October 1955, p. 91.*

WITNESS THAT HE LIVES. I wish to emphasize . . . that
God lives and furthermore, that Jesus is his Beloved Son, the
Savior of the world, and those who have seen Jesus, who

walked with him, who testify of him, as I have narrated, heard him say, "He that hath seen me hath seen the Father."
   —*In Conference Report, October 1959, p. 123.*

REALITY OF CHRIST. The reality of Jesus the Christ must be sensed by you and by me, and the reality of his message must be mine and yours if we hope to advance spiritually and rise above the earth and things which are akin to it. A mere belief in Jesus as a great teacher or even as the greatest man that ever lived has proved inadequate in combating the ills of the world. . . .

The whole philosophy of the progress of man is associated with his divine coming. He is the Son of God, who took upon himself mortality even as you and I, yet divine, even as you and I may become. In the march of this spiritual progress there are certain necessary and definite steps . . .

A *consciousness of freedom*. This is the principle which began when Christ accepted the appointment of his earthly mission. . . .

A *sense of self-mastery*. Before Jesus began his ministry, he proved himself capable of withstanding the tempter. He was tempted yet never once did he yield, and finally declared: " . . . be of good cheer; I have overcome the world." (John 16:33) . . .

A *sense of obligation*. . . . Jesus Christ, as always, is the supreme example. Truly he gave his life for others. "The foxes have holes, and the birds of the air have nests; but the Son of man hath not where to lay his head." (Matt.8:20.) . . .

Consecration to Christ and the right.

When Jesus met the supreme crisis in the Garden of Gethsemane, he said: "Father, . . . not my will, but thine, be done." (Luke 22:42.) This is an example of entire submission of self to the will of God. . . . *Man's highest spiritual achieve-*

ment is to speak and act for the good of his fellow man to the glory of God, and thus make of life a consecrated possession. . . .

The mortal life of Jesus Christ was real. He was born of God: the Babe of Bethlehem, the one perfect Gentleman who ever lived — the Ideal Man whose character was supreme; our Brother, our Savior, the "Anointed One." God help us to make him real in our lives.

—Improvement Era, 64 (1961): 798–99

HAPPINESS IN A KINSHIP WITH CHRIST. Too many men and women have other gods to which they give more thought than to the resurrected Lord — the god of pleasure, the god of wealth, the god of indulgence, the god of political power, the god of popularity, the god of race superiority — as varied and numerous as were the gods of ancient Athens and Rome. . . .

It is therefore a blessing to the world that there are occasions . . . which, as warning semaphores, say to mankind: *In your mad rush for pleasure, wealth, and fame, pause and think what is of most value in life.*

No man can sincerely resolve to apply to his daily life the teachings of Jesus of Nazareth without sensing a change in his own nature. The phrase, "born again," has a deeper significance than many people attach to it. This *changed feeling* may be indescribable, *but it is real.* Happy [is] the person who has truly sensed the uplifting, transforming power that comes from this nearness to the Savior, this kinship to the Living Christ.

—Improvement Era, 65 (1962): 404–5.

THE SHEPHERDS WERE PREPARED. In *Micah*, the fifth chapter, Bethlehem, the City of David, is mentioned by that prophet as the birthplace of the Messiah. I wonder if the shepherds, to whom the revelation of Christ's birth was given, had not that prophecy in mind as they kept watch over their flocks by night.

A revelation of God does not come to man unless he prepares himself for it and lives worthy of it. Evil influences will thrust themselves upon men, but God will be sought. Evil is always crowding and tempting and promising. God asks us to put forth effort and seek: " . . . Seek, and ye shall find; knock, and it shall be opened unto you." (*Matthew* 7:7.) But *we* must seek, *we* must knock; and I think the humble shepherds were treasuring in their hearts the hope, as all Judea was treasuring it, that the Messiah would soon come. Those humble men had opened to them the vision of God.

"And it came to pass, as the angels were gone away from them into heaven, the shepherds said one to another, Let us now go even unto Bethlehem, and see this thing which is come to pass, which the Lord hath made known unto us. (*Luke* 2:15.)

The shepherds did not say, "I wonder if this be true?" They did not say, "Let us go and see if this thing be true." They said, "Let us . . . go . . . and see this thing which is come to pass, which the Lord hath made known unto us"— an assurance that God had revealed His Son; that the angels had given to the world the message that He who would be King of kings, and Lord of lords, had come as a mere babe in the humblest part of that little Judean town. . . .

How can we get that peace of which the angels sang, and which the shepherds found in that little limestone grotto with Mary lying there in a stable; not a stable as we picture it, but a cave in the limestone rock where the animals were kept, near where their keepers slept?

To get that peace is one of the greatest blessings that can come to mortal man. It comes not by lethargy, nor inactivity, but *by doing the Will of God*—that peace which Christ had in mind when after His resurrection He appeared to the Twelve and said ". . . Peace be unto you: . . . " (*John* 20:21.)

This is the message anticipated by the angels who sang: "Glory to God in the highest, and on earth peace, good will toward men." (*Luke* 2:14.)

— Instructor, 97 (1962): 397–98.

EVIDENCES STRONGER THAN SIGHT. On May 5, 1961, Mr. John Cook, a newspaper feature writer, was granted an interview with President McKay. Towards the close of the interview he said that he hoped the President wouldn't mind if he asked a question, and said that the President wouldn't need to answer the question if he felt that he shouldn't, but for his own information, not for publication, he would like to know if President McKay had ever seen the Savior.

President McKay answered that he had not, but that he had heard his voice, many times, and that he had felt his presence and his influence. He then told about Peter (saying that he was his favorite among the apostles, even more so than Paul with all his education and learning—that Peter was a rough, simple man, but sincere) and he told how Peter had spoken of being partakers of the divine spirit, of a divine nature, and explained what he felt that to mean.

Then he told how some evidences were stronger even than that of sight, and recalled the occasion when the Savior appeared to his disciples and told Thomas who had doubted, "Reach hither thy finger and behold my hands: and reach hither thy hand, and thrust it into my side: and be not faithless but believing." And then President McKay said that he liked to believe Thomas did not actually look up, but knelt at the Savior's feet and said unto him, "My Lord and my God." And then President McKay repeated the words of the Master, "Because thou hast seen me, thou hast believed: blessed are they that have not seen, and yet have believed." President McKay then smiled and said, "That is quite a testimony I have given you. I do not know when I have given this before."

— *Ted Cannon, in "Tributes to President David O. McKay,"* Improvement Era, 66 (1963): 785–86.

HEALING IN HIS WINGS. The rising sun can dispel the darkness of night, but it cannot banish the blackness of malice, hatred, bigotry, and selfishness from the hearts of humanity. Happiness and peace will come to earth only as the light of love and human compassion enter the souls of men.

It was for this purpose that Christ, the Son of righteousness, "with healing in his wings," came in the Meridian of Time. Through him wickedness shall be overcome, hatred, enmity, strife, poverty, and war abolished. . . .

Men may yearn for peace, cry for peace, and work for peace, but there will be no peace until they follow the path pointed out by the Living Christ.

— Improvement Era, 67 (1964): 1041–42.

HE WHO RADIATES. The Savior set us the example, always calm, always controlled, radiating something that the people could feel as they passed — the woman who touched his garment is an example. He felt something go from him, that radiation which is divine.

Every man and every person who lives in this world wields an influence, whether for good or for evil. It is not alone what he says, it is not alone what he does — it is what he is. Every man, every person radiates what he or she is.

Every person is a recipient of radiation. The Savior was conscious of that. Whenever he came into the presence of an individual, he sensed that radiation — whether it was the woman of Samaria with her past life; whether it was the woman who was to be stoned, or the men who were to stone her; whether it was the statesman Nicodemus, or one of the lepers.

He was conscious of the radiation from the individual. And to a degree so are you, and so am I. It is what we are and what we radiate that affects the people around us.

—Improvement Era, 69 (1966): 270–71.

MEDITATION. Meditation is one of the most secret, most sacred doors through which we pass into the presence of the Lord. Jesus set the example for us. As soon as he was baptized and received the Father's approval — "This is my beloved Son, in whom I am well pleased" (Matt. 3:17) — Jesus repaired to what is now known as the Mount of Temptation where, during forty days of fasting, he communed with himself and his Father and contemplated the responsibility of his own great mission. One result of this spiritual communion was such strength as enabled him to say to the tempter: "Get thee hence, Satan: for it is written, Thou shalt worship the Lord thy God, and him only shalt thou serve." (Matt. 4:10.)

Before he gave the beautiful Sermon on the Mount, he was in solitude, in communion. He did the same thing after that busy Sabbath day, when he arose early in the morning after having been the guest of Peter. Peter undoubtedly found the guest chamber empty, and when he and others sought Jesus, they found him alone. It was on that morning that they said: "All men seek for thee." (Mark 1:37.)

Again, after Jesus had fed the 5,000 he told the Twelve to dismiss the multitude. Then Jesus, the historian says, went to the mountain for solitude and "when the evening was come, he was there alone." (Matt. 14:23.) Meditation! Prayer!

—Improvement Era, June 1967, p. 80.

THE CENTER OF OUR THOUGHTS AND BEING. Consider the First Article [of Faith]: "We believe in God, the Eternal Father, and in His Son, Jesus Christ, and in the Holy Ghost." If this *belief* has "ripened" into an absolute trust and faith, then intelligence, even what we term "common sense," prompts that we have but one aim or purpose in life; and that is to make Him the center of our thoughts and being—to establish spiritual communion with Him. Material possessions, physical pleasures, become secondary. Our chief goal is to surrender to the Author of our being, our inner life, and to subordinate and to hold in subjection the selfish, sordid pull of nature. Thus, though "having not seen," we can say with equal assurance like Thomas, "My Lord and my God." It then becomes easy to " . . . seek . . . first the kingdom of God and his righteousness." (Matt. 6:33.)

—*Author unlisted*, Our Prophets and Principles (*Salt Lake City: The Instructor, nd*), 4.

WHAT YOU THINK OF CHRIST. What you sincerely think in your heart of Christ will determine what you are, will largely determine what your acts will be. No person can study His divine personality, can accept His teachings, or follow His example, without becoming conscious of an uplifting and refining influence within himself.

—Instructor, *102 (1967): 99.*

REVERENCE, PEACE, AND GOODWILL. As Jesus Christ, our Elder Brother, was born at Bethlehem, "suddenly there was . . . a multitude of heavenly host praising God, and saying:

"Glory to God in the highest, and on earth peace, good will toward men." (Luke 2:13–14.) . . .

Let us consider three principles enunciated at his birth that have marked his mission here upon the earth: first, reverence for God; second, peace; and third, goodwill toward all men—or expressing it another way, godliness, happiness, brotherly kindness.

The first principle, godliness, Jesus exemplified every hour of his earthly existence. On the banks of the Jordan as he was seeking baptism at the beginning of his ministry, we hear him say to John, the forerunner: "Suffer it to be so now: for thus it becometh us to fulfil all righteousness." (Matt. 3:15.)

On the mountain where he was tempted with earthly power and the riches of the world thrown at his feet, we hear him say in sublime majesty, "Get thee behind me, Satan: for it is written, Thou shalt worship the Lord thy God, and him only shalt thou serve." (Luke 4:8.) . . . In the Garden of Gethsemane Jesus prayed: "Father, . . . not my will, but thine, be done." (Luke 22:42.) . . .

The second principle, peace, has been defined as the happy, natural state of man, the "first of human blessings." Without it there can be no happiness. The Prophet Joseph Smith said: Happiness is the object and design of our existence; and will be the end thereof, if we pursue the path that leads to it; and this path is virtue, uprightness, faithfulness, holiness, and keeping all the commandments of God." (*Documentary History of the Church,* Vol. 5, p. 134.)

Jesus said in his Sermon on the Mount: "Blessed are the peacemakers: for they shall be called the children of God." (Matt. 5:9.) . . . Toward the closing scenes of his mortal life, he said to his disciples: "These things I have spoken unto you, that in me ye might have peace. In the world ye shall have tribulation: but be of good cheer; I have overcome the world." (John 16:33.)

On the same occasion he said: "Peace I leave with you, . . . not as the world giveth, give I unto you. Let not your heart be troubled, neither let it be afraid." (John 14:27.)

All through his life peace was on his lips and in his heart, and when he came forth from the tomb and appeared unto his disciples, his first greeting was "Peace be unto you." (John 20:19.)

Peace as taught by the Savior is exemption from individual

troubles, from family quarrels, from national difficulties. Such peace refers to the person just as much as it does to the community. That man is not at peace who is untrue to the whisperings of Christ, the promptings of his conscience. He cannot be at peace when he is untrue to his better self, when he transgresses the law of righteousness, either in dealing with himself, in indulging in passion or appetites, in yielding to the temptations of the flesh, in being untrue to trust, or in transgressing the law of righteousness in dealing with his fellowmen.

The third principle, goodwill, may also be expressed as brotherliness.

Though Jesus gave his message particularly to the chosen house of Israel, he knew no nationality; neither was he a respecter of persons. When the Syro-Phoenician woman came to him in faith, pleading for a blessing for her daughter, he answered, "O woman, great is thy faith: be it unto thee even as thou wilt." (Matt. 15:28) He healed the helpless at the pool of Bethesda. The woman taken in sin was told to go her way and sin no more. . . .

Jesus defeated the lawyer in argument, healed the sick where medicine failed, inspired the greatest music ever written, inspired hundreds of thousands of books, inspired missionaries to go to all the world; yet, in none of the realms in which men and women ordinarily win their laurels do you find historians referring to Christ as having succeeded. But in the realm of character he was supreme!

Jesus the Christ is our Savior, our Mediator with the Father. As the Apostle Paul preached, "Neither is there salvation in any other: for there is none other name under heaven given among men, whereby we must be saved." (Acts 4:12.)

—Improvement Era, *March 1968, pp. 2–3.*

THE RESURRECTION AND THE LIFE. If a miracle is a

supernatural event whose antecedent forces are beyond man's finite wisdom, then the resurrection of Jesus Christ is the most stupendous miracle of all time. In it stand revealed the omnipotence of God and the immortality of man.

The resurrection is a miracle, however, only in the sense that it is beyond man's comprehension and understanding. To all who accept it as a fact, it is but a manifestation of a uniform law of life. Because man does not understand the law, he calls it a miracle. . . .

That the literal resurrection from the grave was a reality to the disciples who knew Christ intimately is a certainty. In their minds there was absolutely no doubt. They were witnesses of the fact. They knew, because their eyes beheld, their ears heard, their hands felt the corporeal presence of the risen Redeemer. . . .

The direct evidence that the tomb did not hold Jesus is threefold: (1) the marvelous transformation in the spirit and work of his disciples; (2) the practically universal belief of the early Church, as recorded in the Gospels; and (3) the direct testimony of Paul, the earliest New Testament writer. . . .

"How can we know the way?" asked Thomas, as he sat with his fellow apostles and their Lord at the table after the supper on the memorable night of the betrayal; and Christ's divine answer was: "I am the way, the truth, and the life. . . . " (John 14:5–6.) And so he is! He is the source of our comfort, the inspiration of our life, the author of our salvation. If we want to know our relationship to God, we go to Jesus Christ. If we would know the truth of the immortality of the soul, we have it exemplified in the Savior's resurrection.

If we desire to learn the ideal life to lead among our fellowmen, we can find a perfect example in the life of Jesus. Whatsoever our noble desires, our lofty aspirations, our ideals in any phase of life, we can look to Christ and find perfection. So, in seeking a standard for moral manhood, we need only to go to the Man of Nazareth and in him find embodied all virtues that go to make the perfect man.

The virtues that combined to make this perfect character are truth, justice, wisdom, benevolence, and self-control. His every thought, word, and deed were in harmony with divine law and, therefore, true. The channel of communication between him and the Father was constantly open, so that truth, which rests upon revelation, was always known to him. . . .

I have cherished from childhood the truth that God is a personal being and is, indeed, our Father whom we can approach in prayer and receive answers thereto. My testimony of the risen Lord is just as real as Thomas', who said to the resurrected Christ when he appeared to his disciples: "My Lord and my God." (John 20:28.) I know that he lives. He is God made manifest in the flesh; and I know that "there is none other name under heaven given among men, whereby we must be saved." (Acts 4:12.)

I know that he will confer with his servants who seek him in humility and in righteousness. I know because I have heard his voice, and I have received his guidance in matters pertaining to his kingdom here on earth.

I know that his Father, our Creator, lives. I know that they appeared to the Prophet Joseph Smith and revealed to him the revelations which we now have recorded in the Doctrine and Covenants and in other Church works. This knowledge is as real to me as that which occurs in our daily lives. When we lay our bodies down at night, we know — we have an assurance — that the sun will rise in the morning and shed its glory over all the earth. So near to me is the knowledge of Christ's existence and divinity of this restored Church.

—Improvement Era, *June 1968, pp. 2–3, 5.*

FELLOWSHIP WITH CHRIST. The Savior, the Son of God, is at the head of this Church . . . —Jesus Christ is our head! I know that the former Presidents of the Church knew that, and declared it. Joseph Smith, the Prophet, knew it. This is Christ's Church, and we are his messengers, his representatives, and it is our duty to keep in touch with him and know what his wishes are. . . . If we keep in tune with Christ and his teachings, we are entitled to fellowship with him. He does not love sin, he does not love lying, nor stealing, misjudging one another, nor condemning others. We have to keep our hearts pure and clean to be worthy of his fellowship.

—Improvement Era, *December 1968, p. 109.*

TESTIMONY OF THE RESURRECTION. I bear my testimony to you and to all the world that The Church of Jesus Christ of Latter-day Saints accepts the resurrection not only as being real, but as the consummation of Christ's divine mission on earth.

I know with my whole soul that as Christ lives after death, so shall all men, each taking his place in the next world for which he has best fitted himself.

—In Conference Report, *April 1969, p. 152.*

Chapter 10

JOSEPH FIELDING SMITH

Born: 19 July 1876
Ordained an Apostle: 7 April 1910
Ordained President: 23 January 1970
Died: 2 July 1972

THE RESURRECTION OF THE PHYSICAL BODY. I have a firm testimony of the mission of our Redeemer, and it is my duty, so far as I have the power, to raise my voice and to declare unto the people, not only of the Latter-day Saints, but in all the world, that Jesus is the Christ, the Son of the living God. . . .

I believe, and you believe, all Latter-day Saints believe, in the literal resurrection of the body and its reuniting with the spirit, thus becoming, as the scriptures inform us, the soul of man. The resurrection of the Son of God was typical. We are informed that his body did not see corruption, although it was placed in the tomb and remained there for the three days. . . . That body was taken up and spirit and body again united inseparably, and in that form he appeared unto his disciples who were unconvinced when he appeared to them and "were terrified and affrighted," the scriptures say, thinking they had seen a spirit. He manifested to them that it was himself, and called upon them, in order to convince them that it was the body that was laid in the tomb, to come and handle him and see for themselves that it was his body that had been pierced and they thrust their hands into the wounds in his hands, his feet and his side.

As he arose from the dead, so shall all men rise; both the just and the unjust shall come forth from the grave. The sea shall give up its dead; the grave shall give up its dead; all shall come forth and stand before the judgment seat of God to be judged according to their works. They shall not all come forth at the same time. Those who are Christ's shall come forth at his coming. . . .

After the resurrection from the dead our bodies will be spiritual bodies, but they will be bodies that are tangible, bodies that have been purified, but they will nevertheless be bodies of flesh and bones, but they will not be blood bodies, they will no longer be quickened by blood but quickened by the spirit which is eternal and they shall become immortal and shall never die. . . .

Paul declared that the body that would be raised would be a spiritual body. You read in the Book of Genesis, where the Lord said to Noah after the flood, that the blood was the life of the body. . . . Therefore, whoso sheddeth man's blood, by man shall his blood be shed, because blood is the life of the mortal body, but with the body brought forth in the resurrection, which is the immortal body, that is not the case, in it blood does not exist, but the spirit is the life-giving power and hence they are no longer bodies quickened by blood but bodies quickened by spirit and hence they are spiritual bodies, but tangible bodies of flesh and bones, just as was the body of the Son of God. Now this is the doctrine of the Lord and Savior of the world.

—In Conference Report, April 1917, pp. 58, 62–63.

REDEMPTION THROUGH CHRIST. I know that Jesus Christ is the Redeemer of the world, that he came into the world to take upon him the transgression of every soul who would repent; and that we, through our repentance and our faith and our acceptance of the principles of the gospel, shall receive full salvation through the shedding of his blood and through the atonement which he brought to pass that we might receive these blessings. Moreover, I know that all men shall be redeemed from death, because men are not responsible for death, therefore Jesus Christ has redeemed them from death through the shedding of his blood. They shall rise in the resurrection, every man to receive his reward according to his works. We who have received the truth of the everlasting gospel ought not to be satisfied with anything short of the best, and the best is the fulness of the Father's kingdom; and for that I hope and pray we shall live and set examples in righteousness to all men that none may stumble, that none may falter, that none may turn from the path of righteousness, due to anything that we may do or say.

—In Conference Report, April 1923, p. 139.

TRUTH ABOUT JESUS CHRIST SHALL ENDURE. If there is any one thing that brings joy and peace and satisfaction to the heart of man, beyond anything else that I know, it is the abiding testimony which I have, and which you have, that Jesus Christ is the Son of God. That is a truth that cannot be changed. Men may attack it; they may ridicule it; they may declare that he is not the Redeemer of the world, that his mission was not true, or that its purpose, through the shedding of his blood, was not to grant unto all men the remission of sins on condition of their repentance. They may refuse to believe in the resurrection from the dead, or even that Christ himself came forth, as the Scriptures declare, after he had been put to death by his enemies; nevertheless the truth remains. He did die for the sins of the world, he did bring to pass redemption from death, he did grant unto men the opportunity of repentance, and remission of sins through their belief and acceptance of the principles of the gospel, and of his mission. These truths are fundamental, they shall endure; they cannot be destroyed no matter what men may say or think.

— In Conference Report, October 1924, pp. 100–101.

HONOR THE FATHER THROUGH THE SON. The Savior taught that no man can testify of God and reject his Son; and that no man can deny that Jesus Christ is the Redeemer of the world and believe in the Father who sent him. We must honor the Father through the Son, and he who rejects the Son and denies the power of the resurrection knows not God. Again the Savior said:

"He that believeth on the Son hath everlasting life, and he that believeth not the Son shall not see life, but the wrath of God abideth on him."

This does not mean that those who reject the Son shall not come forth in the resurrection, for all shall be raised from the dead, but the unbeliever shall not partake of eternal life in the kingdom of God where dwell the Father and the Son. It is, however, the purpose of the Father to extend the power of the resurrection to all men, through the atonement of the Son, and thus give immortality to all his children.

— In Conference Report, April 1926, pp. 40–41.

TO KNOW THEM IN THE FULLNESS. I know . . . God

lives; that Jesus Christ is the Only Begotten Son of God in the flesh, and the Redeemer of the world. But I have not learned all that there is to know about him and our Father, neither have you, for in this mortal life it is impossible for us fully to comprehend the mission of our Lord and Redeemer, to know him and just who and what he is, and the extent of the great work he accomplished. But if we shall be worthy to enter into the presence of God the Father and Jesus Christ his Son and there be crowned with exaltation, it will be necessary for us to know them in the fullness. However, until we do enter into their presence and receive this great blessing, we will not fully know the only true God and Jesus Christ whom he has sent. . . .

When the Savior stood at the well in conversation with the woman of Samaria, he gave her some very important instruction regarding eternal life. There he also declared himself to be the Son of God. He asked her for water to drink, and in turn promised her and all who would believe on him and keep his sayings, that to them he would give water which if they would drink of it they would never thirst. . . .

On another occasion when teaching the Jews, they asked Jesus what sign he could show, or what great work he had accomplished, to prove his ministry. They referred to Moses and to the manna that the Lord had sent to the children of Israel when they were in the wilderness. The Lord answered them thus:

"Verily, verily, I say unto you Moses gave you not that bread from heaven, but my Father giveth you the true bread from heaven.

"For the bread of God is he that cometh down from heaven, and giveth life unto the world."

So he declared himself to be the water of life and the bread of life, and made the promise that those who would receive this water and this bread should never thirst, and never hunger, their souls would be satisfied. They misunderstood him; the woman thought he spoke of water which quenches thirst. The Jews thought he spoke of bread which sustains the body, but he was speaking of the principles of the gospel, these principles of eternal life which, if the people would live them, would bring them back into the presence of the Father. . . .

Those who do not dwell there shall not know them, for they shall not be blessed with eternal life, which is God's life, although they may be in possession of immortality, for all men will receive the gift of the resurrection through the atonement of Jesus Christ. We must have faith in Jesus Christ as the Son of God. We must believe in the Father, in the Son, and in the Holy Ghost, as three separate and distinct personages, the Father and the Son having bodies of flesh and bones, not blood.

   —In *Conference Report*, October 1925, pp. 112, 114–15.

REDEMPTION TO EVERY LIVING THING. I believe in Jesus Christ as the Son of God and the only begotten Son of the Father in the flesh; that he came into the world as the Redeemer, as the Savior; and through his death, through his ministry, the shedding of his blood, he has brought to pass redemption from death to all men, to all creatures—not alone to man, but to every living thing, and even to this earth itself, upon which we stand, for we are informed through the revelations that it too shall receive the resurrection and come forth to be crowned as a celestial body, and to be the abode of celestial beings eternally.

   —In *Conference Report*, October 1934, pp. 64–65.

THE LORD'S METHOD OF ESTABLISHING TRUTH. I recall the remark of one minister who said: "If the plates of such curious workmanship made of gold had been placed in a museum where they could be examined by archaeologists and scientists who could have endorsed them to be what you claim them to be, then all the world would have believed in Joseph Smith. You cannot expect us to accept the story as you tell it to the world."

The answer to all such criticisms is a simple one based on evidence in the Bible. . . . You are all familiar with the story of Lazarus and the rich man as recorded in the sixteenth chapter of Luke. The rich man, after he died, found himself in torment. He plead with Abraham to send Lazarus to his five brothers to check them in their evil course so that they might not come to the place of torment where he was. Abraham said to him: "They have Moses and the prophets; let them hear them." The man replied: "Nay, father Abraham; but if one went unto them from the dead, they will repent." Abraham answered: "If they hear not Moses and the prophets, neither will they be persuaded, though one rose from the dead." . . .

After our Redeemer appeared to the people on this western hemisphere, Mormon records the following:

"And now there cannot be written in this book even a hundredth part of the things which Jesus did truly teach unto the people. . . .

"And these things have I written, which are a lesser part of the things which he taught the people; and I have written them to the intent that they may be brought again unto this people, from the Gentiles, according to the words which Jesus hath spoken.

"And when they shall have received this, which is expedient that they should have, first, to try their faith, and if it shall so be that they shall believe these things then shall the greater things be made manifest unto them.

"And if it so be that they will not believe these things, then shall the greater things be withheld from them, unto their condemnation."

This is the manner in which the Lord deals with mankind,

for he says: "I work not among the children of men save it be according to their faith." It seems very strange that this criticism should be raised so frequently against the Book of Mormon, and yet these same critics never seem to realize that the same procedure always has been followed by the Lord according to the history in the Bible. It is sufficient for our purpose to mention one or two incidents on this point.

When the Savior ministered among men, he said: "I am not sent but unto the lost sheep of the house of Israel," and after his resurrection he did not appear to the high priest and the members of the Sanhedrin, and say to them: "I told you I was the Son of God, and that I would rise from the dead, and you did not believe me." He did not appear to Pilate and say to him: "When you asked me if I am the King of the Jews, I said to you, 'Thou sayest?' and now you will be convinced for I am risen from the dead." He did not appear to any of his enemies; but he did appear to his disciples and commissioned them and sent them forth to declare to the world that he had risen from the dead. It was Peter, James and John and the other apostles who declared to the Jews, after his resurrection: "We are his witnesses," and they were sent to testify to all the world.

To all who offer their criticisms against Joseph Smith for the manner in which the Book of Mormon came forth, we might say in the same sort of criticism: Why did not our Lord appear to the scribes and rulers of the Jews after his resurrection and convince them that he was in very deed the Son of God? Why did he not go to Pilate and set him right and bring him into his fold? What a wonderful thing this would have been. Then all the enemies would have been convinced and his great work would have spread more rapidly, for all men would have believed. This is, as the story of Lazarus proves, foolish reasoning. That is not the way the Lord performs his great work. From the beginning of time he has always presented his message to the world through chosen witnesses. The course followed by Joseph Smith is consistent. He did that which he was commanded. It was the plan before the foundation of the world that in this mortal life men should walk by faith, not by sight, but withal, aided by the sacred word which the Lord would reveal to his servants the prophets.

— 13 August 1944 radio address, in The Restoration of All Things (Salt Lake City: Deseret News Press, 1945?), 103–6.

THE GREAT SUFFERING. We cannot comprehend the great suffering that the Lord had to take upon himself to bring to pass this redemption from death and from sin. He spent a few years upon the earth, and during that short sojourn he suffered the abuse of men. They stoned him; they spat upon him; they cursed him; they ridiculed him; they accused him of almost every crime they could think of, and finally they took him and crucified him upon a cross.

We get into the habit of thinking, I suppose, that his great suffering was when he was nailed to the cross by his hands and his feet and was left there to suffer until he died. As excruciating as that pain was, that was not the greatest suffering that he had to undergo, for in some way which I cannot understand, but which I accept on faith, and which you must accept on faith, he carried on his back the burden of the sins of the whole world. It is hard enough for me to carry my own sins. How is it with you? And yet he had to carry the sins of the whole world, as our Savior and the Redeemer of a fallen world, and so great was his suffering before he ever went to the cross, we are informed, that blood oozed from the pores of his body, and he prayed to his Father that the cup might pass if it were possible, but not being possible he was willing to drink.

— In Conference Report, October 1947, pp. 147–48.

GIFTS OF THE ATONEMENT. There are two great gifts that
come through the atonement of Jesus Christ. The resurrection
of the dead—the defeat of Satan and death, and the restoration
of every creature born into this world to life. That is a gift
that comes without their asking for it. It is one they cannot
refuse to receive. It is not one that they receive by merit. It
is a free gift. It comes to both good and bad alike, not one
soul will fail of the resurrection. If one did, Christ would not
gain the victory and so he redeems every soul from a condition
for which they were not responsible. On the other hand, He
died to redeem only those who are willing to obey His commandments and walk humbly in the light of truth from their
own sins. Every man will pay a price for his own sins who
will not repent and accept Jesus Christ and keep his commandments, the gospel of Jesus Christ.

—*"The Atonement of Jesus Christ," typescript of 25 January 1955 address
at Brigham Young University, p. 6*

THE FIRST VISION. For some fifteen hundred years or
more, perhaps, the world had lost the truth in relation to the
Father and the Son. . . . In the year 325, at a conclave that
was held, they adopted a new idea entirely in regard to God
and confused the Father and the Son, and the Christian world,
from that day down until now, has looked upon the Father
and the Son as being mysterious—I cannot say individuals,
nor can I say substance, but some sort of spirit without sep-
aration[.] And the idea of the separate individuals, Father and
Son, from that day on ceased to exist.

Now, if the Prophet was telling a falsehood when he went
into the woods to pray, he never would have come out and
said that he had seen a vision of the Father and the Son and
that they were separate Personages, and that the Father introduced the Son and then told the Prophet to address his
question to the Son, who would give him the answer. The

Prophet never would have thought of such a thing as that, had it been a fraud.

If he had come out of the woods saying he had seen a vision, had it been untrue never would he have thought of separating Father and Son, nor would he have ever thought of having the Father introduce the Son and for him to put his question to the Son to receive his answer. He never could have thought of it; for that was the farthest thing from the ideas existing in the world in the year 1820.

The very fact that the Prophet made that statement that he saw the Father and the Son and they were glorious Personages, and that the Father spoke to him and introduced the Son, but did not ask him what he wanted, is one of the most significant things that ever occurred in the history of this world. The Prophet, if he had been telling an untruth, even if he had thought that the Father and the Son were separate Personages, would have made another very serious error, if he had lied about it. More than likely he would have said he saw the Father and the Son and the Father asked him what he wanted, and the Father gave him the answer. It would have been fatal to his story. He did not make a mistake. It was Jesus who answered his question, and the Father introduced his Son, just as he did at the baptism of the Savior, and just as he did to the three, Peter, James, and John, on the Mount, and the Savior gave the answer, as all answers have come from our Father in heaven from the beginning, since Adam was driven out of the garden of Eden down to this day. They have all come through the Son. . . .

Do I believe that the Prophet saw the Father and the Son? I certainly do. I know it. I do not need a vision. Reason teaches that to me. And then I have that knowledge also by the guidance of the Spirit of the Lord. The Lord has made it known to me.

—In Conference Report, April 1960, pp. 71–72.

CHRIST THE MEDIATOR. When Adam was in the Garden of Eden, he was in the presence of his Father and received instruction from Him. He knew our Father as we know our fathers in mortal life. When Adam transgressed the law under which he was living, he together with his wife, Eve, was banished from the presence of God. From that day until the last enemy—death—is overcome, Christ stands as the Mediator between man and God, and He is the Advocate for man with the Father. As our Mediator, He labors to bring us into agreement with our Eternal Father.

All revelations, manifestations and commandments, which are received by prophets for the benefit of all people, come though Jesus Christ [Jehovah]. He stands between God the Father and man, and He pleads for man, representing the Father in all commandments given to man and representing man in pleadings to the Father. . . .

Our departed ancestors are not in a position to intercede for us. Christ alone has this right. . . .

We know that the Eternal Father of all has rarely made an appearance, or has seldom been seen or heard by man. In the rare manifestations of the Father, He merely introduced or acknowledged His Son. At no time since the fall of Adam has the Father given commandments directly to the prophets. The deliverance of messages is the office and calling of Jesus Christ as the Messenger, Advocate, and Mediator of the Father. . . .

There is evidence, however, that Christ frequently spoke in the first person, on behalf of the Father, as if the Father himself were speaking. This He did by divine investiture of authority. This right He received from His Father.

—Instructor, 96 (1961): 178.

CHRIST CHOSEN AS OUR REDEEMER. By long and careful observation our Father was able to judge a righteous and unerring judgment in relation to his children. Because of this perfect judgment in that far distant day before the earth on which we now live was formed, the Father chose men according to their ability and talents to be rulers on the earth. Christ, who is the firstborn in the Spirit of the children of God, was elevated to Godhood, and in the vision Abraham saw he describes him as being like unto God. He was chosen, as our scriptures say, as the Lamb slain from before the foundation of the earth. When the plan of salvation and the mortal existence were discussed, he was chosen to be the Only Begotten Son of God on the earth. This was his divine right by birth and appointment of the Father.

— The Progress of Man *(Salt Lake City: Deseret Book Company, 1964),* 74.

THE SECOND COMING OF CHRIST. The Savior taught his disciples that he would come to earth again in the last days in power and great glory to set up his kingdom and bring to pass the end of the world. By end of the world is not meant the end of the earth, but the end of the reign of Satan, or of wickedness. Isaiah by the spirit of prophecy speaks of the second coming, and declares that at that day Christ will come in the clouds of heaven with dyed garments, glorious in his apparel, traveling in the greatness of his strength. And when the inhabitants of the earth ask, "Wherefore art thou red in thine apparel, and thy garments like him that treadeth in the wine vat?" He will answer: "I have trodden the wine press alone: and of the people there was none with me: for I will tread them in mine anger, and trample them in my fury; and their blood shall be sprinkled upon my garments, and I will stain all my raiment. For the day of vengeance is in mine heart, and the year of my redeemed is come." — Isaiah 63:1–4. Compare D. and C. 113:63–74.

Since the fall of Adam and his ejection from the Garden

of Eden, Satan has usurped authority and dominion upon the earth. This he could not have done if the children of Adam had not hearkened to him and followed him in his wickedness. In the wisdom of the Almighty, this domination by the forces of evil with Lucifer at their head has been permitted that men might be tried and proved according to the plan declared before the foundation of the earth was laid. The time is near, even at our doors, when this unrighteous domination of the earth and its inhabitants, governments, kingdoms, and peoples, by Satan shall come to an end. . . . The whole earth is filled with violence which will increase until Christ comes as the Prince of Peace to set all things in order. Shortly after the restoration of the Church, the Lord said:

"For I am no respecter of persons, and will that all men shall know that the day speedily cometh; the hour is not yet, but is nigh at hand, when peace shall be taken from the earth, and the devil shall have power over his own dominion.

"And also the Lord shall have power over his saints, and shall reign in their midst, and shall come down in judgment upon Idumea, or the world."

The time has now come when peace has been taken from the earth, and the devil has, today, power over his own dominion. That dominion will soon cease to be. The other part of this prophecy is about to be fulfilled. The scourge of the Lord is now passing over the nations, as he promised it should in the day of wickedness, "and the report thereof" is vexing all people, but we have been told that "it shall not be stayed until the Lord come." . . .

We have been informed that the place where the Ancient of Days shall sit is Adam-ondi-Ahman, in Missouri. At this place Adam dwelt after he was driven from the Garden of Eden. Here, three years before his death, he called his posterity together, those who were righteous, and blessed them. "And the Lord appeared unto them, and they rose up and blessed

Adam, and called him Michael, the prince, the archangel. In fulfillment of this scene in Daniel's vision, here, once again, Adam—the Ancient of Days—shall come to visit his people at a time when the judgment shall sit, and Christ shall come and receive dominion, and glory, and a kingdom, which shall not pass away, and "all people, nations, and languages, shall serve him." . . .

This gathering of the children of Adam, where the thousands, and the tens of thousands are assembled in the judgment, will be one of the greatest events this troubled earth has ever seen. At this conference, or council, all who have held keys of dispensations will render a report of their stewardship. Adam will do likewise, and then he will surrender to Christ all authority. Then Adam will be confirmed in his calling as the prince over his posterity and will be officially installed and crowned eternally in this presiding calling. Then Christ will be received as King of kings, and Lord of lords. . . .

Following this grand council there shall come upon the earth great changes. In the restoration, spoken by the mouths of all the holy prophets since the world began, the earth is to be renewed and cleansed from all unrighteousness. . . .

The day and the hour of [the Lord's] coming no man knows, neither the angels in heaven, but he will come when the vast majority of mankind are the least prepared for it, and when they are denying his power, saying that he delayeth his coming. It will be a time similar in all respects to the days of Noah, when the great flood swept over the earth. We are informed that it will be in a day when knowledge is increased (Daniel), but also a day when men will be "ever learning, and never able to come to the knowledge of the truth" (Paul).

When Christ took his departure from his disciples and ascended into heaven, two witnesses stood by in white apparel, who said to the disciples: "Ye men of Galilee, why stand ye gazing up into heaven? This same Jesus which is taken up from you into heaven, shall so come in like manner as ye have seen him go into heaven."

John was informed that when Christ should come again it would be to reign upon the earth for one thousand years. . . .

Malachi speaks of the day of the coming of the Lord and declares that it shall burn as an oven and all the proud, yea, and all that do wickedly, shall be stubble: "and the day that cometh shall burn them up, saith the Lord of Hosts, that it shall leave them neither root nor branch." In this manner have all the prophets spoken. Wickedness must come to an end, for it would be inconsistent to have Satan loose seeking to regain his lost power and contending with men, as he has done for six thousand years.

During the earth's Sabbath, the seventh thousand years, which is set apart as the reign of peace and righteousness, Christ will rule undisturbed by any wicked element or influence from the adversary of truth and righteousness. Not only will the earth be cleansed from all wickedness during this reign of peace, but the Church, or kingdom of God now known as the Church, will be cleansed also. The Lord declared it in the following words. "The Son of man shall send forth his angels, and they shall gather out of his kingdom all things that offend, and them which do iniquity."

—The Progress of Man, 476–85.

HE IS AT THE HEAD. I desire to say that no man of himself can lead this church. It is the Church of the Lord Jesus Christ; he is at the head. The Church bears his name, has his priesthood, administers his gospel, preaches his doctrine, and does his work.

He chooses men and calls them to be instruments in his hands to accomplish his purposes, and he guides and directs them in their labors. But men are only instruments in the

Lord's hands, and the honor and glory for all that his servants accomplish is and should be ascribed unto him forever.

If this were the work of man, it would fail, but it is the work of the Lord, and he does not fail. And we have the assurance that if we keep the commandments and are valiant in the testimony of Jesus and are true to every trust, the Lord will guide and direct us and his church in the paths of righteousness, for the accomplishment of all his purposes.

Our faith is centered in the Lord Jesus Christ, and through him in the Father.

—*In Conference Report, April 1970, p. 113.*

TO BE TRIED AND TESTED. The Savior came to earth, not alone to redeem men, but to overcome the world, to gain mortal experiences, to be tried and tested, as is the case with all of us. . . .

Christ did not study chemistry, or physics or sociology in the colleges of his day. Indeed, as we know them, these subjects were neither devised nor taught in his day.

But he did so live as to receive knowledge by revelation from the Holy Ghost, thus setting the pattern for all of us. We are commanded to seek learning, even by study and also by faith. I think we should do all we can during our student years to learn those things which will benefit us during our mortal probations and enable us to have the means and talents to further the Lord's work on earth.

—*Quoted in J.M. Heslop, "USU Students Counseled to Put Spiritual Understanding First," Church News, 16 January 1971, pp. 3, 9.*

FOLLOWING IN HIS FOOTSTEPS. The supreme act of worship is to keep the commandments, to follow in the footsteps of the Son of God, to do ever those things that please him. It is one thing to give lip service to the Lord; it is quite

another to respect and honor his will by following the example
he has set for us. . . .

All my life I have studied and pondered the principles of
the gospel and sought to live the laws of the Lord. As a result
there has come into my heart a great love for him and for his
work and for all those who seek to further his purposes in the
earth.

I know that he lives, that he rules in the heavens above
and in the earth beneath, and that his purposes shall prevail.
He is our Lord and our God. As he himself said to Joseph
Smith: "The Lord is God, and beside him there is no Savior."
—In Conference Report, October 1971, pp. 6–7.

THE LORD DIRECTS US. I think there is one thing which
we should have exceedingly clear in our minds. Neither the
President of the Church, nor the First Presidency, nor the
united voice of the First Presidency and the Twelve will ever
lead the Saints astray or send forth counsel to the world that
is contrary to the mind and will of the Lord. . . .

The Lord is with his people. The cause of righteousness
shall prevail. Our cause is just, and the Lord will guide and
direct us and bring us off triumphant in the end.
—In Conference Report, April 1972, p. 99.

THEY ARE CHRIST'S, AND CHRIST IS GOD'S. The third
and highest kingdom—the celestial—is where God and
Christ dwell. There are, even in this kingdom, different de-
grees of glory, but it is the privilege of every member of the
Church, who will receive and be true to every covenant and
obligation, to gain the exaltation. All who gain the highest
exaltation, the Lord has said, are made "equal in power, and
in might, and in dominion." All power is given unto them,
they become "gods, even the sons of God, wherefore, all things
are theirs, whether life or death, or things present, or things

to come, all are theirs and they are Christ's, and Christ is God's."

— "*The Wisdom of President Joseph Fielding Smith,*" The New Era, *July 1972, p. 22.*

Twilight of Life. As I stand now, in what I might call the twilight of life, with the realization that in a not-far-distant day I shall be called upon to give an account of my mortal stewardship, I bear testimony again of the truth and divinity of this great work.

I know that God lives and that he sent his beloved Son into the world to atone for our sins.

I know that the Father and the Son appeared to the Prophet Joseph Smith to usher in this final gospel dispensation.

I know that Joseph Smith was and is a prophet; moreover, that this is the Lord's church, and that the gospel cause shall roll forward until the knowledge of the Lord covers the earth as the waters cover the sea.

I am sure that we all love the Lord. I know that he lives, and I look forward to that day when I shall see his face, and I hope to hear his voice say unto me: "Come, ye blessed of my Father, inherit the kingdom prepared for you from the foundation of the world." (Matt 25:34.)

— *In Conference Report, October 1971, pp. 178–79.*

Chapter 11

HAROLD B. LEE

Born: 28 March 1899
Ordained an Apostle: 10 April 1941
Ordained President: 7 July 1972
Died: 26 December 1973

STAND AT THE DOOR. The Master said to John, "Behold, I stand at the door and knock and if any man will hear my voice and will open the door, I will come in to him and sup with him, and him with Me." He would bid us all to have in mind that He is not far away. It isn't the Master who keeps Himself from us, but rather we who keep ourselves from Him. Outside of the door of our own soul He is knocking, but we have to hear His voice and we have to open the door before He can come in to help us with our problems. No person ever heard His voice, or had impressions that came from Him, except he was humble in the keeping of the commandments of God, which humility and which obedience entitled him to

166

the companionship of the spirit by which divine truth could
be revealed.

—*"Faith," speech given at Brigham Young University, 28 June 1955,
microfilm, LDS Church Archives, p. 1.*

MY MIND WAS BEING DIRECTED. I was faced with a
difficult, trying problem. I know what Enos means when he
said, "My soul hungered, and I went out by myself where I
could pray." I had a spiritual experience. I saw no light. I
heard no voice to my physical senses, but I knew then as
surely as I know now that I live, that on that night, when I
was struggling, seeking, I had done everything in my power
to prepare myself for the great responsibility that lay ahead.
I knew in my own soul that that night my mind was being
directed by an omnipotent power which pierced my very soul.
And when I read the experience of Elijah the prophet, I knew
what Elijah meant when he related his experience when the
power of the Lord drew near to him.

"And he said, Go forth, and stand upon the mount before
the Lord. And, behold, the Lord passed by, and a great and
strong wind rent the mountains, and brake in pieces the rocks
before the Lord; but the Lord was not in the wind: and after
the wind an earthquake; but the Lord was not in the earthquake:

"And after the earthquake a fire; but the Lord was not in
the fire: and after the fire a still small voice.

"And it was so, when Elijah heard it, that he wrapped his
face in his mantle, and went out, and stood in the entering
in of the cave. And, behold, there came a voice unto him,
and said, What doest thou here, Elijah?" (1 Kings 19:11–
13.) . . .

In all solemnity, and with all my soul, I bear you my
testimony that I know that Jesus lives, that he is the Savior
of the world. I know that he reveals himself and is revealing

himself to his prophets. Week by week, day by day, we see
the on-rolling of his works, guided and directed, and shep-
herded on every side, through the president of the Church,
who has been set apart to preside as the mouthpiece of the
Lord to His Church.

— " 'But Arise and Stand upon Thy Feet' — and I Will Speak with Thee,"
BYU Speeches of the Year, 7 February 1956, pp. 11–12.

TESTIMONY AT THE GARDEN TOMB. As we stood before
the empty tomb in Jerusalem we, too, knew . . . [that] because
of this sacrifice we, too, can have our sins remitted and be
made worthy to stand in his holy presence in the days to
come. . . .

I come away from some of these experiences never to feel
the same again about the mission of our Lord and Savior and
to have impressed upon me as I have never had it impressed
before, what it means to be a special witness. I say to you
with all the conviction of my soul, I know that Jesus lives. I
know that he was the very Son of God.

— "I Walked Today Where Jesus Walked . . . ," BYU Speeches of the
Year, 10 December 1958, p. 12.

OBEDIENCE TO GOD'S WILL. Many times I personally
have wondered at the Master's cry of anguish in the Garden
of Gethsemane. "And he went a little farther, and fell on his
face, and prayed, saying, O my Father, if it be possible, let
this cup pass from me: nevertheless not as I will, but as thou
wilt." (Matt. 26:39.)

As I advance in years, I begin to understand in some small
measure how the Master must have felt. In the loneliness of
a distant hotel room 2,500 miles away, you, too, may one day
cry out from the depths of your soul as was my experience:
"O dear God, don't let her die! I need her; her family needs
her."

Neither the Master's prayer nor my prayer was answered. The purpose of that personal suffering may be only explained in what the Lord said through the Apostle Paul:

"Though he were a Son yet learned he obedience by the things which he suffered;

"And being made perfect, he became the author of eternal salvation unto all them that obey him;" (Heb. 5:8–9.)

So it is in our day. God grant that you and I may learn obedience to God's will, if necessary by the things which we suffer. One of the things that characterizes us as Saints, as King Benjamin told us, was to be "submissive, meek, humble, patient, full of love, willing to submit to all things which the Lord seeth fit to inflict upon him, even as a child doth submit to his father." (Mosiah 3:19.)

—In *Conference Report*, October 1965, pp. 130–31.

CHRIST'S PRESENCE. I have an interesting session with every missionary company in the temple on the fifth floor, in the big assembly room, where they are invited to ask any questions they may wish to ask about the temple ordinances.

In one of these sessions a missionary asked, "Can you tell us a place in this temple where the Lord has appeared?" I suppose he was referring to a testimony that some have borne about someone who had appeared in the temple.

I said, "Now don't look for *a* place. This is the House of the Lord. This is where the Lord comes when he comes to see us on the earth. I imagine he has walked all the halls and every room. He is looking at us; maybe he is here today. I can't imagine a place where he would rather be than right here. Here are 300 or so of you going out on missions to preach his gospel. Maybe he is here with you."

—L. Brent Goates, Harold B. Lee, Prophet and Seer (*Salt Lake City: Bookcraft, 1985*), pp. 391–92.

MORE POWERFUL THAN SIGHT IS THE WITNESS OF THE HOLY SPIRIT. When I came to this position as a member of the Quorum of the Twelve, I was told that my chief responsibility now was to bear testimony of the divine mission of the Lord and Savior of the world. That was almost a crushing realization of what it meant to be a member of the Quorum of the Twelve Apostles. I was assigned to give the Easter talk the Sunday night following the general conference. As I locked myself in one of the rooms of the Church office building, I took out my Bible and read from the four Gospels the life of the Master, particularly leading down to his crucifixion and resurrection. And as I read, I became aware that something different was happening. It no longer was just a story of the doings of the Master, but I realized that I was having an awareness of something I had not had before. It seemed that I was reliving. I was feeling intently the actual experiences about which I was reading. And when I stood that Sunday night, after expressing myself as to the divine mission of the Lord, I said, "And now, as one of the least among you, I declare with all my soul that I know . . . " I knew with a certainty that I had never known before. Whether that was the more sure word of prophecy I had received, I don't know. But it was with such conviction! More powerful than sight is the witness of the Holy Spirit which bears testimony to your spirit that God lives, that Jesus is the Christ, that this is indeed the work of God. I knew it because I had felt it, and there had been a testimony borne to my soul that I could not deny.

—*"Objectives of Church Education," 17 June 1970 address to seminary leaders, Brigham Young University, pp. 7–8, LDS Church Archives.*

I HEARD A VOICE. As a young boy I was out on a farm waiting for my father to finish his day's work, playing about and manufacturing things to wile away the time, when I saw over the fence in the neighbor's yard some broken-down buildings where the sheds were caving in and had rotting timbers. I imagined that that might be a castle that I should explore, so I went over to the fence and started to climb through; then I heard a voice as distinctly as you are hearing mine: "Harold, don't go over there." I looked in every direction to see where the speaker was. I wondered if it was my father, but he couldn't see me. There was no one in sight. I realized that someone was warning me of an unseen danger—whether a nest of rattlesnakes or whether the rotting timbers would fall on me and crush me, I don't know. But from that time on, I accepted without question the fact that there were processes not known to man by which we can hear voices from the unseen world, by which we can have brought to us the visitations of eternity.

On the day when I came to this call, which imposed a greater responsibility to be a witness of the mission of the Lord and Savior Jesus Christ—I suppose no one ever came to such a position without a lot of soul-searching, realizing his own inadequacy, and without the help of the Almighty—after a long night of searching and days of spiritual preparation that followed, I came to know as a witness more powerful than sight, until I could testify with a surety that defied all doubt, that I knew with every fiber of my soul that Jesus is the Christ, the Son of the living God, that he lived, he died, he was resurrected, and today he presides in the heavens, directing the affairs of this church, which bears his name because it preaches his doctrine. I bear that testimony humbly.

—In British Area General Conference Report, August 1971, pp. 141–42.

GUIDE ME, O LORD. These last few weeks have been overwhelming weeks of experience. A number who have interviewed me have said, "You are the head of the Church, aren't you?" and I said, "No, I am not the head of the

Church. The Lord and Savior, Jesus Christ, is the head of this Church. I happen to be the one who has been called to preside over His Church at the present time here upon the earth; but the Master, our Lord and Savior, is the head of this Church." . . .

Someone asked a great surgeon, "How does it feel to have the power of life and death in your hands as you operate?" The surgeon answered, "I never feel that way. When I was a young, cocksure surgeon, I was proud of my ability and my record. Then one day I had to make a hair-breadth decision. I wasn't correct. For some time, I wouldn't operate. As I sat depressed, thinking of my failure, it suddenly came to me, in all humility, that God had given me these hands, had given me these brains, not to be wasted. I prayed to him then to let me have another chance. I still do. I pray each time I take a scalpel in hand, 'Guide my hands, O Lord, and give me of thy knowledge.' You see, he is the famous surgeon, I am only his servant."

He is also the famous architect. He is also the greatest of all teachers. Did you ever think that scientists have discovered anything that God didn't already know? Think of it. He has given you and me hands. He has given you and me brains, and he hasn't given them to us to waste. He expects us to lean on him and exercise to the best of our ability in order to use them righteously in righteous purposes. . . .

As I have sought to live as close as I know how, to know His mind and will concerning matters, and to take the first steps during this last change in the Presidency of the Church, I need your faith and prayers. . . . I plead with you to pray for me, and I promise you that I will try to so live that the Lord can answer your prayers through me. I'll try my best to be your servant.

— 13 August 1972 M-Men and Gleaner fireside address, Salt Lake Tabernacle, microfilm, LDS Church Archives, pp. 1, 4.

DAY BY DAY. I bear you my solemn witness that it is true, that the Lord is in his heavens; he is closer to us than you have any idea. You ask when the Lord gave the last revelation to this Church. The Lord is giving revelations day by day, and you will witness and look back on this period and see some of the mighty revelations the Lord has given in your day and time. To that I bear you my witness.
—In Conference Report, October 1972, p. 131.

"LORD, WHAT WILT THOU HAVE ME DO?" Perhaps even more important than trying to speculate as to what Jesus would do in a given situation is to endeavor to determine what Jesus would have you do. Of course in order to give intelligent answers to such questions, one must have intimate acquaintance with the life of the Master and the account of his ministry and an understanding of the applications he made to the lessons he taught. History, either religious or secular, is valuable to us; for by learning how others adjusted in the past to given situations, we ourselves form patterns of conduct that will guide us to act similarly under similar circumstances. . . .

Before we can feel our kinship to our Savior and be influenced by his teachings in all our thoughts and deeds, we must be impressed by the reality of his existence and the divinity of his mission. . . .

One of the most beautiful pictures of the Master has come down to us in the writings of John the Beloved who was speaking both from his memories of Jesus and from a vision given him wherein the Lord appeared:

"His head and his hairs were white like wool, as white as snow. His eyes were as a flame of fire, and his feet like unto fine brass, as if they burned in a furnace; and his voice was as the sound of many waters; . . . and his countenance was as the sun shineth in its strength. And when I saw him, I fell at his feet as dead. And he laid his right hand upon me, saying,

Fear not; . . . I am he that liveth and was dead." (Revelation 1:14–18.)

Suppose you try to put yourself in the place of one who had received such a visitation from a holy personage. Hardly had the sting of mourning been soothed after the death of Jesus when Mary, fearing that someone had stolen the Master's body from the tomb, was searching for him in the garden. She heard him speak her name and heard him say, "I ascend to my Father and to your Father, to my God and your God." Then she went and told Peter and the disciples as they mourned and wept, "And they, when they had heard that he was alive and had been seen of her believed it not." After that he appeared to two of them near Emmaus in a form that they failed to recognize at first, as they walked and went into the country. (Mark 16:10–12.) He accepted their invitation to "abide with them" when it was eventide and the day was far spent. He sat at meat and gave a blessing on the bread that they ate, and their eyes opened so that they knew him. (Luke 24:29–31.) When they told their experience to the disciples their story was treated as had been the story of Mary Magdalene. He thereafter appeared to the disciples without Thomas being present and again when he was present and quieted their fears with his blessing, "Peace be unto you." Here it was that he "upbraided them with their unbelief and hardness of heart, because they believed not them which had seen him after he was risen." (Mark 16:14.) He invited them to see the prints of the nails in his hands and feet and the wound in his side and to handle him to make them sure of his reality as a tangible resurrected being. (Luke 24:37–41.) He dined on broiled fish and honeycomb with seven of his disciples on the shores of the Sea of Tiberias. After forty days he gathered them together on Mt. Olivet near Jerusalem to witness his ascension and they saw him "taken up, and a cloud received him out of their sight." (Acts 1:9.) But there remained with them the abiding memory of his last words to them, "Lo, I am with you alway, even to the end of the world." (Matt. 28:20.) They knew that he meant what he said.

Perhaps if you, too, were to have such a visitation you would ask as did Saul of Tarsus when the Lord appeared to him on the way to Damascus, "Lord, what wilt thou have me do?" His appearances to his disciples after his resurrection convinced them of his continued existence. Though they could not have him continually in sight after his ascension, there certainly was no confusion in their minds as to the reality of his existence. Never again would they leave their ministry to go fishing without hearing his accusing question, "Lovest thou me more than these?" Peter who shrank from the consequences of revealing his identity at the time of the crucifixion now went unafraid to his ordained responsibilities of leadership and later to a martyr's death without fear because he had seen in the Master the rewards of a just life through a glorious resurrection. Would not the partaking of the sacrament in remembrance of him take on new significance now? How could the two at Emmaus thereafter ask a blessing upon their food and give thanks to God for it without remembering that the resurrected Lord had sat across the table from them and who now though invisible might be very near! No longer could Peter walk alone on the shores of Galilee without a feeling that he was not alone, nor when imprisoned at Antioch by Herod was he greatly surprised when he heard the voice of the angel commanding him to arise quickly, although he was securely bound to two sleeping guards. He never doubted because he knew the power of the risen Lord.

As the Apostle Paul stood before King Agrippa he retold the story of his conversion and of the appearance of the Lord and declared with boldness that now in his ministry he could not be "disobedient unto the heavenly vision." With zeal unbounded and unmindful of personal safety, he labored unceasingly to carry the Gospel to the gentile nations.

And so it was with the Prophet Joseph Smith in our own day, as he declared in his own story to the world: "I had actually seen a light, and in the midst of that light I saw two Personages, and they did in reality speak to me; and though I was hated and persecuted for saying that I had seen a vision, yet it was true; and while they were persecuting me, reviling me, and speaking all manner of evil against me falsely for so saying, I was led to say in my heart: Why persecute me for telling the truth? I have actually seen a vision, and who am I that I can withstand God, or why does the world think to make me deny what I have actually seen? For I had seen a vision; I knew it, and I knew that God knew it, and I could not deny it, nether dared I do it, at least I knew that by so doing I would offend God, and come under condemnation."

After the vision left him, do you think for one moment that although he no longer continued to see the Father and the Son that he was not constantly assured amidst his persecutions and imprisonment that his Heavenly Father was mindful of his every act? With that sublime knowledge, it was only natural that as new problems presented themselves to him in carrying out instructions in the translation of the gold plates and in the setting up of the Kingdom of God on the earth as he was commanded to do, that he turned to the Lord in mighty prayer, and like the brother of Jared spoken of in the Book of Mormon, "Having this perfect knowledge of God he could not be kept from within the veil; therefore he saw Jesus; and he did minister unto him." (Ether 3:20.) One who has such perfect knowledge would, as did the Prophet Joseph or Peter and Paul, walk daily in the company of angels and have conversation with them and receive from them such instructions and authority as are necessary to establish the great work he might be called to do.

Not many have seen the Savior face to face here in mortality, but there is no one of you who has been blessed to receive the gift of the Holy Ghost after baptism but that may have a perfect assurance of his existence as though you had seen. Indeed if you have faith in the reality of his existence even though you have not seen, as the Master implied in his statement to Thomas, that even greater is the blessing to you who "have not seen, and yet have believed" (John 20:29); for "we walk by faith not sight" (II Cor. 5:7), although not seeing, yet believing we rejoice with joy unspeakable in receiving the end of our faith, even the salvation of our souls (I Peter 1:8–9). The testimony of Jesus is the spirit of prophecy (Revelation 19:10), and comes only by the power of the Holy Ghost, for "no man can say that Jesus is the Lord, but by the Holy Ghost" (I Cor. 12:3). If you have lived worthy of such a testimony you may have "a more sure word of prophecy" (II Peter 1:19), by asking God "nothing doubting," and "by the power of the Holy Ghost, ye may know the truth of all things" (Moroni 10:5).

—Decisions for Successful Living (Salt Lake City: Deseret Book Company, 1973), 45–51.

POWERFUL WITNESS. I bear you that sacred testimony, that I know with a witness that is more powerful than sight. Sometime, if the spirit prompts me, I may feel free to tell you more, but may I say to you that I know as though I had seen, that He lives, that He is real, that God the Father and his Son are living realities, personalities with bodies, parts, and passions—glorified beings. If you believe that, then you are safe. If you don't believe it, then struggle for that witness, and all will be well with you.

—"Be Loyal to the Royal within You," in Speeches of the Year: BYU Devotional and Ten-Stake Fireside Addresses 1973 (Provo: Brigham Young University Press, 1974), 103.

THE LORD IS NEAR US. In the closing moments of this conference, I have been moved as I think I have never been moved before in all my life. If it were not for the assurance that I have that the Lord is near to us, guiding, directing, the burden would be almost beyond my strength, but because I know that he is there, and that he can be appealed to, and if we have ears to hear attuned to him, we will never be left alone. . . .

Follow the Brethren; listen to the Brethren. I bear you my witness as one whom the Lord has brought to this place. . . . I thank the Lord that I may have passed some of the tests, but maybe there will have to be more before I shall have been polished to do all that the Lord would have me do.

Sometimes when the veil has been very thin, I have thought that if the struggle had been still greater that maybe then there would have been no veil. I stand by, not asking for anything more than the Lord wants to give me, but I know that he is up there and he is guiding and directing. . . .

Peace be with you, not the peace that comes from the legislation in the halls of congress, but the peace that comes in the way that the Master said, by overcoming all the things of the world. That God may help us so to understand and may you know that I know, with a certainty that defies all doubt that this is his work, that he is guiding us and directing us today, as he has done in every dispensation of the gospel, and I say that with all the humility of my soul, in the name of the Lord, Jesus Christ. Amen.

—In Conference Report, Oct. 1973, p. 170.

TO KNOW NOTHING SAVE JESUS CHRIST. From the beginning of time duly appointed prophets of God have received, as did Moroni, things that were as if in the present; and yet they were not, for Jesus Christ has shown them unto holy men so that they knew of a certainty that which was to come. As the Prophet Amos declared, "Surely the Lord God will do nothing, but he revealeth his secret unto his servants the prophets." (Amos 3:7.)

No event in the history of the world was revealed in greater plainness to the prophets on both the eastern and western hemispheres than was the advent of Jesus the Christ into the world. His identity and his relationship to God, the Eternal Father, and as "the God of this earth," was clearly explained when he as the risen Lord, following his crucifixion and resurrection, appeared to his people in the land Bountiful on this continent.

This is the record:

"And it came to pass that the Lord spake unto them saying:

"Arise and come forth unto me, that ye may thrust your hands into my side, and also that ye may feel the prints of the nails in my hands and in my feet, that ye may know that I am the God of Israel and the God of the whole earth, and have been slain for the sins of the world." (3 Ne. 11:13–14.)

In this, his divine announcement, he has given to the world the sure knowledge that he was a God before he came into the world, differing from the Father in that he did not in the premortal world have a body of flesh and bones as did the Father, until after his mortal life, and that subsequently he received his resurrected body.

As Elder James E. Talmage, one of our esteemed scholars, explained in his commentary *Jesus the Christ,* " . . . God the Eternal Father has manifested Himself to earthly prophets or revelators on very few occasions, and then principally to attest the divine authority of His Son, Jesus Christ." (Page 39.)

This the Father did on the occasion of the baptism of Jesus, when he introduced his Son at the time of his baptism by John the Baptist in these words: "This is my beloved Son, in whom I am well pleased." (Matt 3:17.)

One has but to read again the prophetic words of the Lord

to Adam, Jacob, Abraham, and Moses, and to many others, to know that the Lord has sent into the world in every dispensation and in preparation for his advent the sure knowledge of who he was and of his mission for the redemption of mankind through the plan of salvation, by which all may be saved by obedience to the laws and ordinances of the gospel.

By direct revelation to Isaiah, he told of his birth from the young virgin mother. . . .

That from the age of 12 years, the boy Jesus lived in the shadow of the Almighty, there could be little doubt. . . . "Wist ye not that I must be about my Father's business?" . . .

As the years of his ministry wore on, it became clear to the Jews, who had been seeking for a political leader to lead them from the political oppression that they suffered, that such was not his mission. His entire mission was to emphasize the spiritual side of life and to establish an eternal plan of salvation by which, through his atoning sacrifice, all mankind might be saved. . . . Beyond this, he came as a "Lamb slain from the foundation of the world." (Rev. 13:8.) He came to redeem us from the fall, that he might become the first fruits of the resurrection, that all who slept in their graves might come forth from the grave, "they that have done good, unto the resurrection of life; and they that have done evil, unto the resurrection of damnation." (John 5:28–29.)

In fine, he came to demonstrate to the world that he was the Only Begotten of God in the flesh and to show by his supreme sacrifice that he was in very deed the Redeemer of the world.

In his farewell admonition to the saints on the Western hemisphere after his resurrection and his sojourn among them, the Master summarized to each individual who seeks for salvation the full meaning of his mission. These are the words of the resurrected Lord to the Nephites on this continent in his last recorded sermon:

"And no unclean thing can enter into his kingdom, there-fore nothing entereth into his rest save it be those who have washed their garments in my blood, because of their faith, and the repentance of all their sins, and their faithfulness unto the end.

"Now this is the commandment: Repent, all ye ends of the earth, and come unto me and be baptized in my name, that ye may be sanctified by the reception of the Holy Ghost, that ye may stand spotless before me at the last day.

"Verily, verily, I say unto you, this is my gospel. . . . " (3 Ne. 27:19–21.)

—Ensign, *November 1973, pp. 3–4.*

Chapter 12

SPENCER W. KIMBALL

Born: 28 March 1895
Ordained an Apostle: 7 October 1943
Ordained President: 30 December 1973
Died: 5 November 1985

AND THE BATTLE RAGED ON. I recall two or three years ago, when Brother Lee was giving his maiden address as an Apostle of the Lord Jesus Christ from this stand, he told us of his experience through the night after he had been notified of his call. I think I now know something about the experience he had. I have been going through it for twelve weeks. I believe the brethren were very kind to me in announcing my appointment when they did so that I might make the necessary adjustments in my business affairs, but perhaps they were more inspired to give me the time that I needed of a long period of purification, for in those long days and weeks I did a great deal of thinking and praying, and fasting and praying. There were conflicting thoughts that surged through my mind — seeming voices saying: "You can't do the work. You are not worthy. You have not the ability" — and always finally came the triumphant thought: "You must do the work assigned — you must make yourself able, worthy and qualified." And the battle raged on. . . .

When my feeling of incompetence wholly overwhelmed me, I remembered the words of Nephi when he said: " . . . I will go and do the things which the Lord hath commanded, for I know that the Lord giveth no commandments unto the children of men, save he shall prepare a way for them that they may accomplish the thing which he commandeth them." (I Nephi 3:7.) . . . I have seen the Lord qualify men. In my Church experience I have helped to make many bishops. I have seen them grow and prosper and become great and mighty men in the Church; men who were weak and men who were foolish, and they became strong and confounded the wise, and so I rely upon that promise of the Lord that he will strengthen and empower me that I may be able to do this work to which I have been called.

— *In Conference Report, October 1943, pp. 15–16, 18.*

THE SAVIOR OF MANKIND. I read recently in a local paper of a pastor of a church in Illinois, who said that he felt the same reverence for Santa Claus that he did for Jesus Christ. He said:

"I consider both of them to be folk tales, but in different categories."

He finds one difference, however; he does not question the fact that "a *man* named Jesus" did exist, and he regards Santa Claus as a "figure of the imagination."

In the magazine, *Time*, in a recent issue, a noted professor emeritus in one of our largest universities, was quoted at length on his rationalizing. To Jesus of Nazareth he gives human warmth; a great capacity for love; unusual understanding. He calls him a great humanist, a great teacher, a great dramatist. As a typical rationalization, he explains that Lazarus was not dead, but was merely " . . . brought 'back to health' by Jesus, the power of mind and learning, and by the 'therapy of his own abundant vitality!' "

I want to bear testimony today that Jesus is not only a great teacher, a great humanist, and a great dramatist, but is in very deed, the Son of the Living God, the Creator, the Redeemer of the world, the Savior of mankind. I want to testify further that he not only lived in the Meridian of Time for approximately thirty-three years, but that he lived eternities before this, and will live eternities beyond it.

—In Conference Report, October 1946, pp. 55–56.

FOLLOW HIM. The Lord is at the helm, . . . and he will continue to be there, and his work will go forward. The important question is whether we, as individuals, will be going in that same direction. It's up to us.

—In Conference Report, April 1951, p. 104.

CONSIDER YOUR HEROES. Think of the individual who impresses you most as perfection in chastity, cleanliness of mind and of heart and of body, in thought and in deed.

Now think of the one who is most unselfish, whose life is bound up in the lives of others, who thinks little of self and much of associates; one who has made great sacrifices and has suffered and been deprived to give to others.

Now let pass in review one who is your ideal in kindliness, who forgives with all the heart, who carries no bitterness, no envy, no jealousy.

Now . . . who is the individual whom you admire most as one who is obedient, tractable and accountable, who is not servile but humble and free from arrogance and rebellion, who fears God and obeys His laws and commandments, who is devout yet not fanatic, who prays with most sincerity and who follows righteous teachings most completely.

And now consider the person whom you most admire; who is alert of mind, who is keen in intellect, who is great in perception, whose wisdom and judgment are supreme, who knows much but is ever learning; and the individual who is most unselfish, who gives himself, his time, his talents generously for others, who gives and does not get.

And now, the one who exhibits the greatest degree of love — love for the Lord, love for his fellowmen, love for his associates, his family; the one who is gracious, personable, generous, loving; the ideal son, father, daughter, mother and friend.

And now . . . combine all these heroic people with all their monumental virtues into one composite figure and you still have an inferior to the Lord, Jesus Christ, who had all virtues at their best, than whom there is no peer except His Father, God.

— *"An Address by Elder Spencer W. Kimball to the Jordan Seminary Graduation Class in the Jordan High School Auditorium on May 14, 1954," Sandy, Utah, pamphlet, pp. 9–10.*

I THINK HE SMILES. In my own office at home and at the Church Office Building I have rather large pictures of Jesus as he has been portrayed by artists. I appreciate them, but they do not give me the complete or acceptable picture of the Lord, and no picture I have ever seen is adequate. I can never see the Christ with my eyes open. I must close them to get my concepts of him. . . .

I think of the Lord as he walked through Galilee and Palestine. I realize that he must have become tired and hungry and weary and thirsty, but he was ever patient. He was loving; he was kind. It seems that though it was necessary at times to rebuke people, he did what he told us in the modern revelations to do, he reproved then showed forth afterwards an increase of love toward him he had reproved (see D&C 121:43) — he had his arm around them, too. O how I love him for his tenderness — so forgiving, so kind.

I think of him on the cross during his great agony. He was thinking of his sweet mother down beneath him. He was tender and kind as he said to John, "Behold thy mother," and to his mother, "Woman, behold thy son!" (See John 19:26–27.) And from that hour that disciple took her into his own home.

I think of his kindness when proud and loving mothers so wanted their children to have a sight of the Master, to touch the hem of his garment, and they were pushed away — (I think of that incident at the conclusion of nearly every session of conference as we go out the back door and people crowd around to just see and speak to Christ's modern prophet—) and he said, "Suffer the little children to come unto me, and forbid them not: for of such is the kingdom of God." (Mark 10:14.)

I think of the Christ who came in our own day to the Prophet Joseph Smith and his associate in the Kirtland Temple. . . .

"I am the first and the last; I am he who liveth, I am he who was slain; I am your advocate with the Father." (D&C 110:4.)

Several have said no one ever saw Him laugh; however, I can imagine the Lord Jesus Christ smiling as he looked upon his people in their devotion. This great conference — with its thirty-one thousand men and boys holding the Holy Priesthood, in attendance at one meeting; with its tens of thousands who have come long distances to listen and to worship together, and to hear the word of the Lord Jesus Christ — must have pleased him greatly.

I think he smiles when he looks upon this his prophet, President David O. McKay, who gives such inspired leadership to his people, who is so close to him, who hears his word, and who receives his revelations. I think the Lord Jesus Christ is smiling when he looks into the homes of this people and sees them on their knees in family prayer night and morning, the children participating also. I think he smiles when he sees young husbands and wives, and older ones, with deep affection for each other, who continue their courtship as our prophet has said, who continue to love each other with all their souls until the day they die and then accentuate it through eternity. . . .

I think the Lord Jesus Christ is smiling when he looks down and sees more than four thousand men . . . with some of their wives and some of their children who were inactive a year ago, but today are happy in the kingdom, many of whom have been to the holy temple of God and had their endowments and their sealings, and who with tears of gratitude thank the Lord for his program.

I think I see tears of joy in his eyes and a smile on his lips as he sees the twenty-one thousand new souls who have come unto him this year, who have professed his name, who have gone into the waters of baptism, and I think he loves those who helped to convert them also.

I see him smile as he sees his numerous people on their knees in repentance, changing their lives, making them brighter and cleaner, and more like their Heavenly Father and their Brother, Jesus Christ.

I think he is pleased and smiles as he sees youth as they organize their lives and protect and fortify themselves against the errors of the day. I think he is first grieved, and then perhaps pleased, when he sees, as he must have done a few days ago in my office, a young couple who had made serious error and were now on their knees together with their hands tightly clasped together. There must have been joy in his smile when he saw into their souls and saw that they were making

the adjustment, as their tears bathed my hand which I had
tenderly placed on theirs.

Oh, I love the Lord Jesus Christ. I hope that I can show
to him and manifest my sincerity and devotion. I want to live
close to him. I want to be like him.

— In Conference Report, April 1956, pp. 119–20.

A VISIT TO THE HOLY LAND. To visit the places where
such momentous happenings affected the eternities of us all
was most interesting and intriguing and added color to our
picture, but we did not need to walk through the Holy Land
to know eternal truth.

We realized it is not so important to know whether Mt.
Hermon or Mt. Tabor was the transfiguration place but to
know that on the summit of a high mountain was held a great
conference of mortal and immortal beings where unspeakable
things were said and authoritative keys were delivered and
approval was given of the life and works of his only Begotten
Son, when the voice of the Father in the overshadowing cloud
said: "This is my Beloved Son, in whom I am well pleased."
(Matt. 17:5.)

Not so important to know upon which great stone the
Master leaned in agonizing decision-prayers in the Garden of
Gethsemane, as to know that he did in that area conclude to
accept voluntarily crucifixion for our sakes. Not so needful to
know on which hill his cross was planted nor in what tomb
his body lay nor in which garden he met Mary, but that he
did hang in voluntary physical and mental agony; that his
lifeless, bloodless body did lie in the tomb into the third day
as prophesied, and above all that he did emerge a resurrected
perfected one — the first fruits of all men in resurrection and
the author of the gospel which could give eternal life to obedient man.

Not so important to know where he was born and died

and resurrected but to know for a certainty that the Eternal, Living Father came to approve his Son in his baptism and later in his ministry, that the Son of God broke the bands of death and established the exaltation, the way of life, and that we may grow like him in knowledge and perfected in eternal life. And this I know and give my solemn witness.

—In *Conference Report*, April 1961, p. 81.

IN THE PRESENCE OF GOD. To know God, one must be aware of the person and attributes, power, and glory of God the Father and God the Christ. Moses declares he " . . . saw God face to face, and he talked with him . . . " (Moses 1:2.) This experience of Moses is in harmony with the scripture, which says:

"For no man has seen God at any time in the flesh, except quickened by the Spirit of God. Neither can any natural man abide the presence of God, neither after the carnal mind." (D&C 67:11–12. Italics added.)

It must be obvious then that to endure the glory of the Father or of the glorified Christ, a mortal being must be translated or otherwise fortified. Moses, a prophet of God, held the protecting Holy Priesthood: " . . . and the glory of God was upon Moses; therefore Moses could endure his presence." (Moses 1:2.) . . .

A heavenly visitor identified himself to Abraham: "I am the Lord, thy God; I dwell in heaven. . . .

"My name is Jehovah. . . . " (Abraham 2:7–8.)

And Abraham: " . . . talked with the Lord, face to face, as one man talketh with another; . . .

"And he said unto me: My son, my son . . . And he put his hand upon mine eyes, and I saw those things which his hands had made . . . and I could not see the end thereof." (Ibid., 3:11–12.) . . .

Saul of Tarsus saw Jehovah, the glorified Christ, and heard

his voice and conversed with him. Even partially protected as he was, the brilliance of the light from heaven in which he centered— greater than the noonday sun—Paul collapsed to the earth, trembling, shocked. The voice said: "I am Jesus whom thou persecutest. . . . " (Acts 9:5.) . . .

Joseph had had the same general experience of Abraham and Moses and Enoch who had seen the Lord and heard his voice. In addition, he heard the Father, bearing witness of the Son, as had Peter, James, and John on Transfiguration's Mount. He had seen the person of Elohim. He had fought a desperate battle with the powers of darkness as had Moses and Abraham. And like them all, he was protected by the glory of the Lord. This young man gave a new concept to the world. Now at least one person knew God without question, for he had seen and heard. . . .

Men who know God and love him and live his commandments and obey his true ordinances may yet in this life, or the life to come, see his face and know that he lives and will commune with them.

—Improvement Era, 67 (1964): 497–99.

CHRIST CANNOT FORGIVE ONE IN SIN. Apparently the death penalty was still on the law books in the days of Christ, for the scribes and Pharisees brought to the Lord the woman taken in adultery, seeking to trap him. They said Moses had commanded that such a person should be stoned to death, and asked him what he had to say of the matter. With his usual sublime understanding he put the tempters to rout and sent the woman to repent of her sin. (See John 8:1–11.) . . .

Note that the Lord did not forgive the woman of her serious sin. He commanded quietly, but forcefully, "Go, and sin no more." Even Christ cannot forgive one in sin. The woman had neither time nor opportunity to repent totally. When her preparation and repentance were complete she could hope for forgiveness, but not before then. . . .

When we think of the great sacrifice of our Lord Jesus Christ and the sufferings he endured for us, we would be ingrates if we did not appreciate it so far as our power made it possible. He suffered and died for us, yet if we do not repent, all his anguish and pain on our account are futile. In his own words:

"For behold, I, God, have suffered these things for all, that they might not suffer if they would repent;

"But if they would not repent they must suffer even as I.

"Which suffering caused myself, even God, the greatest of all, to tremble because of pain, and to bleed at every pore, and to suffer both body and spirit. . . . " (D&C 19:16–18.)

Abinadi expressed the danger of delaying repentance:

"But remember that he that persists in his own carnal nature, and goes on in the ways of sin and rebellion against God, remaineth in his fallen state and the devil hath all power over him. Therefore, he is as though there was no redemption made, being an enemy to God; and also is the devil an enemy to God." (Mos. 16:5.)

This only underlines the vital importance of repenting *in this life*, of not dying in one's sins.

—The Miracle of Forgiveness (*Salt Lake City: Bookcraft, 1969*), 68, 145.

THE SAVIOR'S EXAMPLE IN RESISTING TEMPTATION. The importance of not accommodating temptation in the least degree is underlined by the Savior's example. Did not he recognize the danger when he was on the mountain with his fallen brother, Lucifer, being sorely tempted by that master tempter? He could have opened the door and flirted with danger by saying, "All right, Satan, I'll listen to your proposition. I need not succumb, I need not yield, I need not accept—but I'll listen."

Christ did not so rationalize. He positively and promptly closed the discussion, and commanded: "Get thee hence, Satan," meaning, likely, "Get out of my sight—get out of my presence—I will not listen—I will have nothing to do with you." Then, we read, "the devil leaveth him."

This is our proper pattern, if we would prevent sin rather than be faced with the much more difficult task of curing it. As I study the story of the Redeemer and his temptations, I am certain he spent his energies fortifying himself against temptation rather than battling with it to conquer it.

—Miracle of Forgiveness, 216-17.

I KNOW THAT HE LIVES. I know that the Lord lives— that God who was with Adam, that God who came to the banks of the Jordan River to say, "This is my beloved Son, in whom I am well pleased" (Matt. 3:17), to introduce his Son to a world that was to depend so completely on him. I know that was the God that we worship, who came on the Mount of Transfiguration and said again to those servants, Peter, James, and John, who were to carry on the work of the Lord even in their imperfections: "This is my beloved Son, in whom I am well pleased" (Matt. 17:5), the same God— we know he lives and exists—who came in the state of New York and said those same things that he had already said to the Nephites—and now said to a world that had been traveling in darkness for a long, long time—"This is My Beloved Son. Hear him!" (Joseph Smith 2:17.)

I know that Jesus is the Christ, the Son of the living God. I know that. I know that the gospel which we teach is the gospel of Jesus Christ and the church to which we belong is the church of Jesus Christ; it teaches his doctrines and his policies and his programs. I know that if all of us will live the

program as he has given it and will continue to give it, that all the blessings promised will be ours.
  —In Conference Report, October 1974, pp. 162–63.

THE LORD'S CONCERN. I know that God lives. I know that Jesus Christ lives. I know that he loves. I know that he inspires. I know that he guides us. And I know that he loves us. I know that he can love or he can feel greatly aggrieved when he sees us getting off the path which he has marked so plainly and made so straight.
  —In Conference Report, April 1975, p. 162.

HE KNOWS WHAT HE IS DOING. Recently a prominent doctor, knowing of my surgery and cancer treatments, exhibited a little surprise at my assuming the great responsibility of the church presidency. He was not a member of the Church and evidently had never known the pull and the pressure one feels when one has a positive assurance that the Lord is *not* playing games, but rather has a serious program for man and for his glory. The Lord knows what He is doing, and all His moves are appropriate and right.

And I was surprised also that any man would wonder and question the work of the Lord. We who have the positive assurance and testimony of the divinity of this work do not question the ways or determinations of the Lord.

I know without question that God lives and have a feeling of sorrow for those people in the world who live in the gray area of doubt, who do not have such an assurance.

I know that the Lord Jesus Christ is the Only Begotten Son of our Heavenly Father, and that He assisted in the creation of man and of all that serves man, including the earth and all that is in the world. He was the Redeemer of mankind and the Savior of this world and the author of the plan of salvation. . . .

I know that the Lord has contact with his prophets, and that he reveals the truth today to his servants as he did in the days of Adam and Abraham and Moses and Peter and Joseph and the numerous others throughout time. . . .

There have been many times when man would not listen, and, of course, where there is no ear, there is no voice.

—*In Conference Report, October 1976, p. 164.*

IT WAS HE. It was He, Jesus Christ, in his glorified state who came to the ancestors of the Indians, who is variously known by them as the Great White Spirit, the Fair God and numerous other names.

It was He, Jesus Christ, our Savior, who was introduced to surprised listeners at Jordan (see Matt 3:13–17), at the holy Mount of Transfiguration (see Matt 17:1–9), at the temple of the Nephites (see 3 Ne. 11–26), and in the grove of Palmyra, New York (see Joseph Smith 2:17–25); and the introducing person was none other than his actual Father, the holy Elohim, in whose image he was and whose will he carried out. . . .

It is noteworthy that the Father, God, Elohim came to the earth upon each necessary occasion to introduce the Son to a new dispensation, to a new people; then Jesus Christ, the Son, carried forward his work.

—*Ensign, November 1977, p. 73.*

COME, FOLLOW ME. Jesus knew who he was and why he was here on this planet. That meant he could lead from strength rather than from uncertainty or weakness. . . .

Jesus said several times, "Come, follow me." His was a program of "do what I do," rather than "do what I say." His innate brilliance would have permitted him to put on a dazzling display, but that would have left his followers far behind. He walked and worked with those he was to serve. His was not a long-distance leadership. He was not afraid of close friendships; he was not afraid that proximity to him would disappoint his followers. The leaven of true leadership cannot lift others unless we are with and serve those to be led. . . .

The Savior's leadership was selfless. He put himself and his own needs second and ministered to others beyond the call of duty, tirelessly, lovingly, effectively. So many of the problems in the world today spring from selfishness and self-centeredness in which too many make harsh demands of life and others in order to meet their demands. This is a direct reversal of the principles and practices pursued so perfectly by that perfect example of leadership, Jesus of Nazareth. . . .

Jesus had perspective about problems and people. He was able to calculate carefully at long range the effect and impact of utterances, not only on those who were to hear them at the moment, but on those who would read them 2,000 years later. So often, secular leaders rush in to solve problems by seeking to stop the present pain, and thereby create even greater difficulty and pain later on. . . .

Jesus was not afraid to make demands of those he led. His leadership was not condescending or soft. . . .

The scriptures contain many marvelous case studies of leaders who, unlike Jesus, were not perfect but were still very effective. It would do us all much good if we were to read them—and read them often. . . .

Perhaps the most important thing I can say about Jesus Christ, more important than all else I have said, is that he lives. He really does embody all those virtues and attributes the scriptures tell us of. If we can come to know that, we then know the central reality about man and the universe. If we don't accept that truth and that reality, then we will not have the fixed principles or the transcendent truths by which to live out our lives in happiness and in service. In other words, we will find it very difficult to be significant leaders unless we

recognize the reality of the perfect leader, Jesus Christ, and let him be the light by which we see the way!
   —Ensign, *August 1979, pp. 5–7.*

SERVE AND LEAD AS CHRIST DID. Much of this special Church work will be judged by the way in which we serve and lead, in a Christ-like manner, the women of the Church who are in our homes. I say serve and lead because the headship of the man in the home is to be like the headship of Christ in the Church. Christ led by love, example, and selfless service. He sacrificed himself for us. So it must be if we are leader-servants and humble patriarchs in our homes. . . .

   I know that God lives, . . . (it is a great joy to say that many, many times), that Christ, the Redeemer of the world, is our Lord, and that this is his Church, The Church of Jesus Christ of Latter-day Saints, with Christ at its head.
   —*In Conference Report, October 1979, pp. 71–72.*

SWEEP OF THE SAVIOR'S LABORS. Only when we understand the ministry of Jesus Christ, in which he also had a preeminence in the premortal world, do we begin to get some sense of the sweep of the Savior's labors for and in behalf of all of us. . . .

   The more one understands about the ministry of Jesus Christ, the more absurd it is to regard him as any less than the resurrected Son of God. . . .

   It is equally important for all of us who are disciples and followers of the Savior, Jesus of Nazareth, to live in such a way that our very lives are a witness by our works and our words that we are indeed believers. . . . May I assure you of the everlasting significance of your personal life. And even though at times the range of your life may seem to be very small, there can be greatness in the quality of your life. . . .

   Those of us today who are sustained by you as prophets,

seers, and revelators came to feel in the spring of 1978 much as the early brethren did when the revelation came to the effect "that the Gentiles should be fellowheirs . . . and partakers of his promise in Christ by the gospel" (Eph. 3:6). . . .

We had the glorious experience of having the Lord indicate clearly that the time had come when all worthy men and women everywhere can be fellowheirs and partakers of the full blessings of the gospel. I want you to know, as a special witness of the Savior, how close I have felt to him and to our Heavenly Father as I have made numerous visits to the upper rooms in the temple, going on some days several times by myself. The Lord made it very clear to me what was to be done. We do not expect the people of the world to understand such things, for they will always be quick to assign their own reasons or to discount the divine process of revelation.

—The New Era, *April 1980, pp. 33–36.*

AT THE SESQUICENTENNIAL. Let us hold fast to the iron rod. The Savior urged us to put our hand to the plow without looking back. In that spirit we are being asked to have humility and a deep and abiding faith in the Lord and to move forward — trusting in him, refusing to be diverted from our course, either by the *ways* of the world or the *praise* of the world. I see that quality of readiness and devotion in our people today. There is so much yet to be done! Let us, then, move forward; let us continue the journey with lengthened stride. The Lord will lead us along, and he will be in our midst and not forsake us.

I know with all my soul that Jesus Christ is the Son of God, that he died on the cross and was resurrected from the dead. He is the risen Lord, the Great Presiding High Priest, and he stands at the head of the Church. Of this I testify . . . on this great anniversary of the restoration and organization of the Church on this very spot 150 years ago.

—In *Conference Report, April 1980, p. 111.*

MY FRIEND, MY SAVIOR, MY LORD, MY GOD. There are some in the world who mistakenly say that we are a non-Christian Church — a cult; that we worship Joseph Smith rather than our Savior, Jesus Christ. How far from the truth they are! What heresy! The Lord declared, "For thus shall my church be called in the last days, even The Church of Jesus Christ of Latter-day Saints" (D&C 115:4).

We have a hope in Christ here and now. He died for our sins. Because of Him and His gospel, our sins are washed away in the waters of baptism; sin and iniquity are burned out of our souls as though by fire; and we become clean, we have a clear conscience, and we gain that peace which passeth understanding. . . .

For the past century and a half since the Restoration, beginning with the Prophet Joseph Smith, the latter-day prophets of God have raised their voices in clarity and with authority and truth as they have borne their testimonies of the divinity of this great latter-day work and the redemptive power of the gospel of Jesus Christ.

To the testimonies of these mighty men I add my testimony. I know that Jesus Christ is the Son of the living God and that He was crucified for the sins of the world. He is my friend, my Savior, my Lord, and my God.

—In Conference Report, October 1982, pp. 5–6.

Chapter 13

EZRA TAFT BENSON

Born: 4 August 1899
Ordained an Apostle: 7 October 1943
Ordained President: 10 November 1985

THE GREATEST EVENT. There is nothing in history to equal that dramatic announcement "He is not here, but is risen."

The greatest events of history are those which affect the greatest number for the longest periods. By this standard, no event could be more important to individuals or nations than the resurrection of the Master. The eventual resurrection of every soul who has lived and died on earth is a scriptural certainty. And surely there is no event for which one should make more careful preparation.

Nothing is more absolutely universal than the resurrection. Every living being will be resurrected. " . . . as in Adam all die, even so in Christ shall all be made alive." (1 Cor. 15:22) . . .

Yes, the Lord Jesus Christ liberated man from the world, by the pure gospel of love. He demonstrated that man, through a love of God, and through kindness and charity to his fellows, could achieve his highest potential. He lived the plain and sure doctrine of service, of doing good to all men, friends and enemies alike. His charge to return good for evil is still the greatest challenge to the mind of man. At the same time it is man's greatest weapon.

No other single influence has had so great an impact on this earth as the life of Jesus Christ. We cannot conceive of our lives without his teachings. Without him we would be lost in a morass of beliefs and worships born in fear and darkness, where the sensual and materialistic hold sway.

We are far short of the goal he set for us, but we must never lose sight of it. Nor must we forget that our great climb toward the light — toward perfection — would not be possible except for his teachings, his life, his death, and his resurrection. . . .

I give you my solemn witness and testimony that I know that Jesus the Christ lives. He was in very deed raised from the dead, as we shall be. He is the "resurrection and the life."

He appeared unto many in the old world after his resurrection.

And according to modern scriptures, sacred to me, he spent three glorious days, before his ascension, with his "other sheep" here in America — the new world.

By him, and through him and his gospel, God the Father has made it possible for you and me to overcome the world. . . .

Jesus is the Christ. He lives. He did break the bonds of death. He is our Savior and Redeemer, the very Son of God.

And he will come again — " . . . this same Jesus, which is

taken up from you into heaven, shall so come in like manner as ye have seen him go into heaven." (Acts 1:11.)

—*29 March 1959 Easter sunrise service address, Hollywood Bowl, California, in* So Shall Ye Reap: Selected Addresses of Ezra Taft Benson, *comp. Reed A. Benson (Salt Lake City: Deseret Book Company, 1960), 4–9.*

DOORS WILL OPEN. Following the glorious appearance of God the Father and his Son Jesus Christ to Joseph Smith, it appears that the first great responsibility placed upon the restored Church was to carry the gospel to the world—to all our Father's children. . . .

The time must surely come when the Iron Curtain will be melted down and the Bamboo Curtain shattered. What the Lord has decreed will be fulfilled. To members of the Church and honest-hearted people everywhere, we remind you that God is at the helm—he is not dead—and he has said, "Be still, and know that I am God." (Ps. 46:10.)

—*Improvement Era, 7 June 1970, pp. 95–96.*

GIFTS OF LOVE. I would like to talk to you about a few of the many gifts we have received from our Lord, Jesus Christ, and what we in turn might give to him.

First, he gave us the perfect model—himself—after which we are to pattern our lives. He said, "Greater love hath no man than this, that a man lay down his life for his friends" (John 15:13). Not only did he lay down before us the perfect example for earthly living, but for our sake he willingly gave us his life. He went through an agony both in body and spirit, of which we cannot comprehend, to bring to us the glorious blessing of the Atonement and the Resurrection (see D&C 19:15–19).

Some men are willing to die for their faith but will not fully live for it. Christ both lived and died for us. . . .

That man is greatest and most blessed and joyful whose

life most closely fits the pattern of the Christ. This has nothing to do with earthly wealth, power, or prestige. The only true test of greatness, blessedness, joyfulness is how close a life can come to being like the Master, Jesus Christ. . . .

I testify to you that his pay for his work is the best pay that you can get in this world or any other.

Secondly, . . . he has provided us the gift of a prophet. Of all mortal men, we should keep our eyes most firmly fixed on the captain, the prophet, seer, and revelator, and President of The Church of Jesus Christ of Latter-day Saints. . . . A good way to measure your standing with the Lord is to see how you feel about, and act upon, the inspired words of his earthly representative, the Prophet-President. . . .

The most important prophet, so far as we are concerned, is the one who is living in our day and age. This is the prophet who has today's instructions from God to us. God's revelation to Adam did not instruct Noah how to build the ark. . . .

Thirdly . . . is the gift of his church, The Church of Jesus Christ of Latter-day Saints, "the only true and living Church upon the face of the whole earth" (D&C 1:30). . . . It is the organized means which God is using to establish and expand his work. We must work with it and in it, build it up and move it forward. . . .

Sometimes in our attempts to mimic the world, contrary to the prophet's counsel, we run after the world's false educational, political, musical, and dress ideas. New worldly standards take over, a gradual breakdown occurs, and finally, after much suffering, a humble people are ready to be taught once again a higher law. . . .

Fourthly . . . is the gift of scripture, particularly the Book of Mormon. . . .

I have noted within the Church the difference in discernment, in insight, in conviction, and in spirit between those who know and love the Book of Mormon and those who do not. That book is a great sifter.

Fifth . . . is the gift of his Constitution. The Lord said, "I established the Constitution of this land, by the hands of wise men whom I raised up" (D&C 101:80). . . .

Christ's great gift to us was his life and sacrifice — should that not then be our small gift to him — our lives and sacrifices, not only now, but in the future? . . .

Men and women who turn their lives over to God will find out that he can make a lot more out of their lives than they can. He will deepen their joys, expand their vision, quicken their minds, strengthen their muscles, lift their spirits, multiply their blessings, increase their opportunities, comfort their souls, raise up friends, and pour out peace. . . .

To gain eternal life, they must be willing, if called upon, to sacrifice all things for the gospel. "If thou wilt be perfect," Jesus said to the rich young man, "go and sell that thou hast, and give to the poor, and thou shalt have treasure in heaven: and come and follow me." . . .

Why don't we go all the way with the Lord — not part way? Why don't we sacrifice all of our sins — not some of them?

She was a young girl. She had sacrificed her worldly plans to spend long, tedious hours in work in order to provide for and raise her younger orphan brother. But now she lay on her bed, dying of a sickness. She called for her bishop, and as she talked to him in her last moments, he held her rough, hard, work-calloused hand in his. Then she asked the question "How will God know that I am his?"

Gently he raised her wrist and answered, "Show him your hands."

Someday we may see that pair of hands that sacrificed so much for us. Are our hands clean, and do they show the signs of being in his service? Are our hearts pure and filled with his thoughts?

Each week we make a solemn covenant to be like him and take him for our leader, to always remember him in everything and keep all of his commandments. In return he promises to give us his Spirit.

—*"Jesus Christ — Gifts and Expectations,"* in Speeches of the Year: BYU Devotional and Ten-Stake Fireside Addresses 1974 *(Provo: Brigham Young University Press, 1975), 301–5, 307, 310, 312–13.*

FORTIFIES TESTIMONY. The Book of Mormon brings men to Christ through two basic means. First, it tells in a plain manner of Christ and his gospel. It testifies of his divinity and of the necessity for a Redeemer and the need of our putting trust in him. It bears witness of the Fall and the Atonement and the first principles of the gospel, including our need of a broken heart and a contrite spirit and a spiritual rebirth. It proclaims we must endure to the end in righteousness and live the moral life of a Saint.

Second, the Book of Mormon exposes the enemies of Christ. It confounds false doctrines and lays down contention. (See 2 Ne. 3:12.) It fortifies the humble followers of Christ against the evil designs, strategies, and doctrines of the devil in our day. The type of apostates in the Book of Mormon are similar to the type we have today.

—*In Conference Report, April 1975, pp. 94–95.*

JESUS VISITED THE SPIRIT WORLD. Even before the fall of Adam, which ushered death into the world, our Heavenly Father had prepared a place for the spirits who would eventually depart this mortal life. At the time of Jesus' death, the spirit world was occupied by hosts of our Father's children who had died — Adam's posterity down to the death of Jesus, both the righteous and the wicked. There were two grand divisions in the world of the spirits. Spirits of the righteous (the just) had gone to paradise, a state of happiness and a place of peace and restful work. The spirits of the wicked (the unjust) had gone to prison, a state of darkness and misery (see Alma 40:12–15.) Jesus went only to the righteous — to paradise.

— "*Because I Live, Ye Shall Live Also,*" in 1978 Devotional Speeches of the Year: BYU Devotional and Fireside Addresses *(Provo: Brigham Young University Press, 1979), 48.*

THE DIVINE BIRTH. The most fundamental doctrine of true Christianity is the divine birth of the child Jesus. It is a doctrine not comprehended by the world, misinterpreted by the so-called Christian churches, and even misunderstood by some members of the true church. . . .

Thus the testimonies of appointed witnesses leave no question as to the paternity of Jesus Christ. God was the Father of His fleshly tabernacle and Mary, a mortal woman, was His mother. He is therefore the only person born who rightfully deserves the title the Only Begotten Son of God.

We must keep in mind who Jesus was before He was so born. He was the Creator of all things, the great Jehovah, the Lamb slain before the foundation of the world, the God of Abraham, Isaac, and Jacob. He was and is the Holy One of Israel. . . .

But because His Father was God, Jesus Christ . . . was God in the flesh — even the Son of God. [His] powers enabled Him to accomplish miracles, signs, wonders, the great atonement, and the resurrection — all of which are additional marks of His divinity. . . .

Jesus Christ is the Son of God in the most literal sense. The body in which He performed His mission in the flesh was sired by that same Holy Being we worship as God, our Eternal Father. He was not the son of Joseph, nor was He begotten by the Holy Ghost. He is the Son of the Eternal Father! . . .

I gratefully bear testimony to the marks which bear witness

to His divinity: His divine birth, His ministry, His resurrection, His atoning sacrifice, His promised coming.
  — The New Era, *December 1980, pp. 45–50.*

MARK OF DIVINITY. Jesus' entire ministry was a mark of
His divinity. He spoke as God, He acted as God, and He
performed works that only God Himself can do. His works
bear testimony to His divinity.

It was in Gethsemane that Jesus took on Himself the sins
of the world, in Gethsemane that His pain was equivalent to
the cumulative burden of all men, in Gethsemane that He
descended below all things so that all could repent and come
to Him.

The mortal mind fails to fathom, the tongue cannot express, the pen of man cannot describe the breadth, the depth,
the height of the suffering of our Lord — nor His infinite love
for us. . . .

As I contemplate the glorious atonement of our Lord,
which extended from Gethsemane to Golgotha, I am led to
exclaim with reverence and gratitude:

> *I stand all amazed at the love Jesus offers me,*
> *Confused at the grace that so fully he proffers me;*
> *I tremble to know that for me he was crucified,*
> *That for me a sinner, he suffered, he bled and died.*
>
> *I marvel that he would descend from his throne divine*
> *To rescue a soul so rebellious and proud as mine,*
> *That he should extend his great love unto such as I,*
> *Sufficient to own, to redeem, and to justify.*
>
> *Oh, it is wonderful that he should care for me,*
> *Enough to die for me!*
> *Oh, it is wonderful, wonderful to me.*
>
> *Hymns, no. 193*

  — Come unto Christ *(Salt Lake City: Deseret Book Company, 1983),*
6–9.

A Testimony of Jesus. A testimony is one of the few possessions we may take with us when we leave this life. Let me explain what it means to have a testimony of Jesus.

To have a testimony of Jesus is to possess knowledge through the Holy Ghost of the divine mission of Jesus Christ.

A testimony of Jesus is to know the divine nature of our Lord's birth—that He is indeed the Only Begotten Son of God in the flesh.

A testimony of Jesus is to know that He was the promised Messiah and that while He sojourned among men He accomplished many mighty miracles.

A testimony of Jesus is to know that the laws He prescribed as His doctrine are true and then to abide by those laws and ordinances.

A testimony of Jesus is to know that He voluntarily took upon Himself the sins of all mankind in the Garden of Gethsemane, which caused Him to suffer in both body and spirit and to bleed from every pore. All this He did so that we would not have to suffer, if we should repent. (See Doctrine and Covenants 19:16, 18.)

A testimony of Jesus is to know that He came forth triumphantly from the grave with a physical, resurrected body. And because He lives, so shall all mankind.

A testimony of Jesus is to know that God the Father and His Son, Jesus Christ, did indeed appear to the Prophet Joseph Smith to establish a new dispensation of His gospel so that salvation may be preached to all nations before He comes.

A testimony of Jesus is to know that the church He established in the meridian of time and restored in modern times is, as the Lord has declared, "the only true and living church upon the face of the whole earth." (Doctrine and Covenants 1:30.)

A testimony of Jesus is to receive the words of His servants, the prophets, for as He has said, "Whether by mine own voice or by the voice of my servants, it is the same." (Doctrine and Covenants 1:38.)

A testimony of Jesus means that we accept the divine mission of Jesus Christ, embrace His gospel, and do His works. It means we accept the prophetic mission of Joseph Smith and his successors. . . .

To walk in the steps of Jesus is to emulate His life and to look unto Him as our source of truth and example. Each of us would do well to periodically review His teachings in the Sermon on the Mount so that we are totally familiar with His way. In that sermon, one of the greatest of all sermons, we are told to be a light to others, to control our anger, to reconcile bad feelings with others before bringing gifts to the Lord, to love our enemy, to refrain from unholy and unvirtuous practices, to not allow lust to conceive in our hearts. We are further instructed how to pray, how to fast, and how to regulate our priorities. When these teachings are applied, Jesus said, we are like the wise man who built his house on a firm, solid foundation. . . .

In the Savior's time the purpose of a yoke was to get oxen pulling together in a united effort. Our Savior has a great cause to move forward. He has asked all of us to be equally yoked together to move His cause forward. It requires not only a united effort; it requires also complete dependence on Him. As He said to His early apostles, "Without me ye can do nothing." (John 15:5.)

—Come unto Christ, 11–13, 37, 97.

CENTER CONFIDENCE, HOPE, AND TRUST IN CHRIST. I desire to bear witness to the divinity of Jesus Christ and to show by His deeds and honored titles given by His Father and the prophets that He is indeed deserving of our love, our reverence, and our worship.

The fundamental principle of our religion is faith in the

Lord Jesus Christ. Why is it expedient to center confidence, hope, and trust in one solitary figure? Why is faith in Him so necessary to peace of mind in this life and hope in the world to come? . . .

Jesus Christ was and is the *Lord God Omnipotent.* . . .

Jesus Christ is the *Son of God.* . . .

His unique heredity made Him heir to the honored title *the Only Begotten Son of God in the flesh.* As the Son of God, He inherited powers and intelligence that no human has ever had before or since. He was literally Immanuel, which means "God with us." . . .

To qualify as the *Redeemer* of all our Father's children, Jesus had to be perfectly obedient to all the laws of God. . . .

As the great *Lawgiver,* He gave laws and commandments for the benefit of all our Heavenly Father's children. . . .

Appropriately I praise Him as the *Rock of Our Salvation.* . . .

We may never understand nor comprehend in mortality *how* He accomplished what He did, but we must not fail to understand *why* He did what He did.

All that He did was prompted by His unselfish, infinite love for us. . . .

He is the *Resurrection* and the *Life.* . . .

He is our *Great Exemplar.*

He was perfectly obedient to our Heavenly Father and showed us how to forsake the world and keep our priorities in perspective. Because of His love for us, He showed us how to rise above petty weaknesses and to demonstrate affection, love, and charity in our relationships with others.

He is the *Bread of Life.* . . .

He is the *Prince of Peace,* the ultimate *Comforter.* . . .

He is the *Good Shepherd.* . . .

He is a *Wonderful Counselor.* . . .

He is our *Advocate, Mediator,* and *Judge.* . . .

With all my soul, I love Him.

He is the same loving, compassionate Lord today as when He walked the dusty roads of Palestine. He is close to His servants on this earth. He cares about and loves each of us today. Of this we can be assured.

—Come unto Christ, *127–33.*

FROM THE INSIDE OUT. When you choose to follow Christ, you choose to be changed. . . .

The Lord works from the inside out. The world works from the outside in. The world would take people out of the slums. Christ takes the slums out of people, and then they take themselves out of the slums. The world would mold men by changing their environment. Christ changes men, who then change the environment. The world would shape human behavior, but Christ can change human nature.

—Ensign, *November 1985, pp. 5–6.*

A BLESSING. I want you to know that I know that Christ is at the helm. This is His world. This is His Church. His purposes will be accomplished. . . .

Now, in the authority of the sacred priesthood in me vested, I invoke my blessing upon the Latter-day Saints and upon good people everywhere.

I bless you with increased discernment to judge between Christ and anti-Christ. I bless you with increased power to do good and to resist evil. I bless you with increased *understanding* of the Book of Mormon. I promise you that from this moment forward, if we will daily sup from its pages and abide by its precepts, God will pour out upon each child of Zion and the Church a blessing hitherto unknown — and we will plead to the Lord that He will begin to lift the condemnation — the scourge and judgment. Of this I bear solemn witness.

—Ensign, *May 1986, pp. 77–78.*

FOLLOW THE PROPHET. These are they who are valiant in their testimony of Jesus, who, as the Lord has declared, "overcome by faith, and are sealed by the Holy Spirit of promise, which the father sheds forth upon all those who are just and true." (D&C 76:53.)

"Those who are just and true!" What an apt expression for those valiant in the testimony of Jesus. They are courageous in defending truth and righteousness. These are members of the Church who magnify their callings in the Church (see D&C 84:33), pay their tithes and offerings, live morally clean lives, sustain their Church leaders by word and action, keep the Sabbath as a holy day, and obey all the commandments of God.

To these the Lord has promised that "all thrones and dominions, principalities and powers, shall be revealed and set forth upon all who have endured valiantly for the gospel of Jesus Christ." (D&C 121:29.) . . .

One who rationalizes that he or she has a testimony of Jesus Christ but cannot accept direction and counsel from the leadership of His church is in a fundamentally unsound position and is in jeopardy of losing exaltation.

—Ensign, *February 1987, p. 2.*

ANOTHER TESTAMENT OF JESUS CHRIST. The honest seeker after truth can gain the testimony that Jesus is the Christ as he prayerfully ponders the inspired words of the Book of Mormon.

Over one-half of all the verses in the Book of Mormon refer to our Lord. Some form of Christ's name is mentioned more frequently per verse in the Book of Mormon than even in the New Testament.

He is given over one hundred different names in the Book of Mormon. Those names have a particular significance in describing His divine nature.

Let us consider some of the attributes of our Lord, as found in the Book of Mormon, that show that Jesus is the Christ. Then let us confirm each of these attributes about Him with a brief quote from the Book of Mormon.

He is *Alive:* "The life of the world . . . a life which is endless" (Mosiah 16:9).

He is *Constant:* "The same yesterday, today, and forever" (2 Nephi 27:23).

He is the *Creator:* "He created all things, both in heaven and in earth" (Mosiah 4:9).

He is the *Exemplar:* He "set the example. . . . He said unto the children of men: Follow thou me" (2 Nephi 31:9, 10).

He is *Generous:* "He commandeth none that they shall not partake of his salvation" (2 Nephi 26:24).

He is *Godly:* He is God (see 2 Nephi 27:23).

He is *Good:* "All things which are good cometh of God" (Moroni 7:12).

He is *Gracious:* "He is full of grace" (2 Nephi 2:6).

He is the *Healer:* The "sick, and . . . afflicted with all manner of diseases . . . devils and unclean spirits . . . were healed by the power of the Lamb of God" (1 Nephi 11:31).

He is *Holy:* "O how great the holiness of our God!" (2 Nephi 9:20)

He is *Humble:* "He humbleth himself before the Father" (2 Nephi 31:7).

He is *Joyful:* "The Father hath given" Him a "fulness of joy" (3 Nephi 28:10).

He is our *Judge:* We "shall be brought to stand before the bar of God, to be judged of him" (Mosiah 16:10).

He is *Just:* "The judgments of God are always just" (Mosiah 29:12).

He is *Kind:* "He has loving kindness . . . towards the children of men" (1 Nephi 19:9).

He is the *Lawgiver:* He "gave the law" (3 Nephi 15:5).

He is the *Liberator:* "There is no other head whereby ye can be made free" (Mosiah 5:8).

He is the *Light:* "The light . . . of the world; yea, a light that is endless, that can never be darkened" (Mosiah 16:9).

He is *Loving:* "He loveth the world, even that he layeth down his own life" (2 Nephi 26:24).

He is the *Mediator:* "The great Mediator of all men" (2 Nephi 2:27).

He is *Merciful:* "There is a multitude of his tender mercies" (1 Nephi 8:8).

He is *Mighty:* "Mightier than all the earth" (1 Nephi 4:1).

He is *Miraculous:* A "God of miracles" (2 Nephi 27:23).

He is *Obedient:* Obedient unto the Father "in keeping his commandments" (2 Nephi 31:7).

He is *Omnipotent:* He has "all power, both in heaven and in earth" (Mosiah 4:9).

He is *Omniscient:* "The Lord knoweth all things from the beginning" (1 Nephi 9:6).

He is our *Redeemer:* "All mankind were in a lost and in a fallen state, and ever would be save they should rely on this Redeemer" (1 Nephi 10:6).

He is the *Resurrection:* He brought to pass "the resurrection of the dead, being the first that should rise" (2 Nephi 2:8).

He is *Righteous:* "His ways are righteousness forever" (2 Nephi 1:19).

He is the *Ruler:* He rules "in the heavens above and in the earth beneath" (2 Nephi 29:7).

He is our *Savior:* "There is none other name given under heaven save it be this Jesus Christ . . . whereby man can be saved" (2 Nephi 25:20).

He is *Sinless:* "He suffereth temptation, and yieldeth not to the temptation" (Mosiah 15:5).

He is *Truthful:* "A God of truth, and canst not lie" (Ether 3:12).

He is *Wise:* "He has all wisdom" (Mosiah 4:9). . . .

Those who are committed to Christ "stand as witnesses of God at all times and in all things, and in all places" that they may be in "even until death" (Mosiah 18:9). They "retain the name" of Christ "written always" in their hearts (Mosiah 5:12). They take upon themselves "the name of Christ, having a determination to serve him to the end" (Moroni 6:3).

—Ensign, *November 1987, pp. 83–84.*

THE GREATEST BATTLES. Great battles can make great heroes and heroines. We will never have a better opportunity to be valiant in a more crucial cause than in the battle we face today and in the immediate future. Some of the greatest battles we will face will be fought within the silent chambers of our own souls. . . .

Christ lived on earth and was subject to all manner of temptation, but He won every battle. He is the most successful warrior that ever walked the earth, and He wants to help us win every battle, be it personal or public. When we fall short, His atonement will compensate for us on condition of our repentance.

—Ensign, *September 1988, p. 2.*

I TESTIFY OF CHRIST. I testify that in our premortal state our Elder Brother in the spirit, even Jesus Christ, became our foreordained Savior in the Father's plan of salvation. (See Mosiah 4:6–7; Alma 34:9.) He is the captain of our salvation and the only means through whom we can return to our Father in Heaven to gain that fulness of joy. (See Heb. 2:10; Mosiah 3:17; Alma 38:9.)

I testify that Lucifer was also in the council of heaven. He sought to destroy the agency of man. He rebelled. (See

Moses 4:3.) There was a war in heaven, and a third of the hosts were cast to the earth and denied a body. (See Rev. 12:7–9; D&C 29:36–37.) Lucifer is the enemy of all righteousness and seeks the misery of all mankind. (See 2 Ne. 2:18, 27; Mosiah 4:14.) . . .

I testify that God reveals His will to all men through the Light of Christ. (See Moro. 7:16; D&C 93:2; John 1:9.) . . .

I testify that Christ was born into mortality with Mary as His mother and our Heavenly Father as His father. (See 1 Ne. 11:18–21; Mosiah 3:8.) He lived a sinless life, providing us a perfect example. (See D&C 45:4; 3 Ne. 12:48; 27:27.) He worked out the great Atonement, which, through His grace, provides for every soul a resurrection and, for the faithful, the means to become exalted in the celestial kingdom. (See A of F 3; 2 Ne. 25:23; Mosiah 4:6–7; Alma 11:41–45; D&C 76:50–70; 132:19.)

I testify that during His mortal ministry Christ established His church on the earth. (See Matt. 16:18; Acts 2:47; 3 Ne. 21:22.) He called and ordained men to be Apostles and prophets with authority so that what they bound on earth would be bound in heaven. (See Matt. 16:19; John 15:16.) They received revelation, which provided new scriptures. (See 2 Pet. 1:20–21; D&C 68:4.)

I testify that a world so wicked that it killed the Son of God soon began killing the Apostles and prophets and so plunged itself into a spiritual dark age. (See 2 Thess. 2:2–7.) Scripture ended, apostasy spread, and the church that Christ established during His earthly ministry ceased to exist. (See 2 Ne. 27:4–5.)

I testify that God the Father and His Son, Jesus Christ, appeared to Joseph Smith in the spring of 1820, thus bringing to an end the long night of apostasy (JS–H 1:15–20). . . .

I testify that through the Book of Mormon God has provided for our day tangible evidence that Jesus is the Christ and that Joseph Smith is His prophet. (See D&C 20:8–33.) This other testament of Jesus Christ is a scriptural account of the early inhabitants of America. It was translated by Joseph Smith through the gift and power of God. (See D&C 135:3.) Those who will read and ponder the Book of Mormon and ask our Eternal Father in the name of Christ if it is true may know for themselves of its truthfulness through the power of the Holy Ghost, provided they will ask with a sincere heart, with real intent, having faith in Christ. (See Moro. 10:3–5.) . . .

I testify that as the forces of evil increase under Lucifer's leadership and as the forces of good increase under the leadership of Jesus Christ, there will be growing battles between the two until the final confrontation. . . .

I testify that not many years hence the earth will be cleansed. (See D&C 76:41.) Jesus the Christ will come again, this time in power and great glory to vanquish His foes and to rule and reign on the earth. (See D&C 43:26–33.) In due time all men will gain a resurrection and then will face the Master in a final judgment. (See 2 Ne. 9:15, 41.) God will give rewards to each according to the deeds done in the flesh. (See Alma 5:15.)

I testify to you that a fulness of joy can only come through the atonement of Jesus Christ and by obedience to all of the laws and ordinances of the gospel, which are found only in The Church of Jesus Christ of Latter-day Saints. (See A of F 1:3.)

—In Conference Report, October 1988, pp. 102–4.

INDEX

217